Wild Dogs

LIONCREST
PUBLISHING

WILD DOGS
An Adventure in Adolescence

ISBN   978-1-5445-2197-8   *Hardcover*
       978-1-5445-2196-1   *Paperback*
       978-1-5445-2198-5   *Ebook*
       978-1-5445-2318-7   *Audiobook*

Wild Dogs

An Adventure in Adolescence

Christos Kalogirou

This book is dedicated to Hounds, past, present, and future.

My book. Our stories.

Contents

Dear reader,

Mandi Schwartz was a student at Athol Murray College of Notre Dame. She was on a path to great things as a hockey player and a Yale University pre-med student when she was diagnosed with acute myeloid leukemia, more commonly known as bone marrow cancer. Mandi was a schoolmate, and while she fought tirelessly to beat the disease, she unfortunately lost her cancer battle on April 3, 2011.

Inspired by her consistently optimistic attitude, from the first day of her diagnosis to her final days on this earth, Mandi's family and friends raised an international profile around the ease and importance of joining the bone marrow registry. Anyone wishing to be considered as a bone marrow donor can participate by simply contributing cells collected with a mouth swab.

Through the ongoing efforts of Mandi's family and friends and others like them, countless matches have been identified and lives saved. This ripple effect, inspired by Mandi and carried forth by so many, is seen every day by the mothers, fathers, sons, daughters, and other family members whose loved ones are still alive today because of these efforts.

All proceeds from the sale of *Wild Dogs* are being donated to the Mandi Schwartz Foundation and to a bursary in her name.

Mandi's Foundation: Mandi17.org

Join the registry in the USA: Join.BeTheMatch.org

Join the registry in Canada: Blood.ca/StemCells

Thank you for purchasing this book and for your kind contribution to the foundation.

Sincerely,

Christos Kalogirou

Foreword

By Terry O'Malley

Three-time Olympian (1964, 1968, and 1980); teacher and
hockey and lacrosse coach, 1978–2003; President, Athol
Murray College of Notre Dame, 2003–2006

 arrived at Athol Murray College of Notre Dame in the fall of 1978. At the time, the school infrastructure was in pretty rough shape. Martin Kenney, whose son Jason Kenney would later become the Premier of Alberta, was president of the college. Martin was on the verge of rebuilding its structure, enrollment, reputation, and organization. Looking back more than forty years, it's been an exciting journey.

As I read through this journal of Christos Kalogirou's exploits at Notre Dame, I was reminded of the time my brother, affectionately known as Uncle Mike, came to visit our family at Wilcox.[1] It was a snowfall year to remember, with drifts up to the roof of our home. He started to build snow forts with our children. It didn't take the students long to see this as a new opportunity. Later in that term, out behind the Max Bell dormitory, the dorm parents found an enormous snow fort with adjoining tunnels forming a large chamber filled with rugs, furniture, and candles. An ingenious structure, it was the extra-curricular meeting place for contraband participation.

Notre Dame's Christos Kalogirou's plan was ingenious too. It was just a few generations down the highway. Christos dedicates his story to the many Hounds, the brothers and sisters who have experienced living in residence at Notre Dame.

These exploits and incidents are not in the brochures!

As you read Christos's account of his time at Notre Dame, bear in mind that the staff wasn't unaware of the goings-on among the students; it is just that there is a time-lapse in catching up to the imagination of a teenager. It's like a scene from 1939 described in Jack Gorman's seminal book on the college, *Père Murray and the Hounds*: "Suddenly, the front door burst open and a tall, gangly kid came running out.... In hot pursuit was a stocky, angry little man in short sleeves.... Finally, the boy outdistanced him.... 'One of these days I'll catch up with that little bastard and give him a good kick in the ass,' the man said."[2] That man was Père Athol Murray.

Yes, "catching up" is ongoing.

The year 2020 marked the 100th Anniversary of Athol Murray College of Notre Dame, located forty-three kilometers south of Regina, Saskatchewan. I wrote a decade-by-decade introduction for Notre Dame's centennial picture album. It is a story of faith, risk, courage, hardship, hard work, and community cooperation to manage a century of education. It was suggested to me by a visitor to the school that Notre Dame was like a hummingbird. Aerodynamically, it should not be able to fly, but because it works so hard, it manages.

Notre Dame continues to manage because of a loyal alumni and board. The teachers and staff often put in twice the forty-hour week in academic, extracurricular activity, administration, and dormitory duty. The college chases excellence. About a hundred students make honor roll, and all students participate in the school's outreach program. The artwork produced by May Homecoming Weekend is exceptional. Some years, the school has eleven hockey teams; some seasons, Notre Dame students compete in all seventeen high school provincial championships.

Feeding more than 300 students three times a day is no little thing. Athol Murray led by example. He taught four classes a term and ministered to three parishes, along with his administrative responsibilities, which included finding the funds to cover food and pay salaries. The Sisters of Charity of St. Louis, the first educators there in 1920, did likewise. They were heroic characters in the pioneering days of settlement in Saskatchewan.

Athol Murray and the Sisters had hopes for their students. A 1933 brochure directed them as follows: "Under God, take the initiative, give back to the community, and look for a chivalrous project for your life." The school's motto is "Struggle and Emerge."

Ideals are always lofty. Three times a day in the foyer of Varsity Hall,[3] students walk by a bronze plaque outlining the ideal education. It is taken from the playbook of Notre Dame of Indiana, an education that has served Western civilization for millennia. The plaque states:

That Notre Dame, under the guidance of Almighty God, may serve, in the generations to come, the highest interests of mankind by drawing into a common fellowship the members of the faculty and the student body, by gathering into a true society of teacher and student, the graduate and the undergraduate; further, that the members of Notre Dame may discover within its walls the true education that is to be found good fellowship, in friendly disputation and debate, in the conversation of wise and prudent men and women, in music, in pictures and the play, in the casual book, in sports and games and the mastery of the body, and lastly, that

Notre Dame may be dedicated to the task of arming youth with strength and suppleness of limb, with clarity of mind and depth of understanding, and with a spirit of true religion and high endeavor.

This is what is in the brochures!

The late Jimmy Williams, a "one of a kind" college librarian at Notre Dame, encouraged Christos to tell "his own story." Jimmy used to say, "It would be a pretty boring place without some kangaroos bouncing around. You have to give them a chance."

Some students go directly after their goals, others tack like a sailor, or as some ND staff would say: "they are on the four-year plan." Christos was on the four-year plan. Most of his story is about his community life outside of structured classrooms and activities. There used to be a daily American radio storytelling with host Paul Harvey. He had millions of followers and would sign off with his trademark: "and that's the rest of the story."

That's what we have here.

We are all aware that education has a formal and informal side to it. When I looked at the recent Notre Dame web page, there was a section where students suggested what the school means to them. Most suggested it was the friendships gained by hanging out in the dorms and around the campus, sharing ups and downs, riding the buses—all places where conversation occurs and bonds are built. This meaning was more to them than personal goals of school grades or making a team or championships. It is the sense of belonging to the Notre Dame family.

Like any family, Notre Dame has boundaries and expectations. There is a "grid book" for discipline too. The college has tried to create a more family-oriented atmosphere in the dormitory life by putting houseparent residences at the end of each dorm. The houses were divided by color and names used during WWII: Gunners, Badgers, Woodchoppers, and Marauders. Discipline involved hours of service around the college and workouts. Some students got to love the workouts so much that they would swear when a houseparent would come into the room just to hear the words: "Give me fifty!" And down they'd go and rattle off fifty pushups. They were proud of their athleticism. The staff always preferred students who, when caught breaking the rules, just did the discipline and then got on with their year.

It has been an evolutionary move from the raw English boarding school model to today. There is a "survival" side to living in school dormitories too. It is why the college moved grade-nine students into separate dorms—they needed more attention and protection. Grade-twelve students had a separate dorm as the pressure to graduate with good marks required different study rules. But it was really hard to break the "old boy, new boy" culture from self-service to service to the school. Finally, the college put all new students together in rooms and all returning students together. These things helped, but as in any group dynamic, one has to stand up for oneself. And, if you were too smart by one half, expect a dressing down by your peers and teachers. Christos calls it having "street smarts."

As Christos goes on with his time at Notre Dame, what better way to make yourself indispensable to your peers than to supply contraband liquor to fellow students. The story of how Christos tried to manage this, as well as proactively gained his place at the college, reads along quickly with all the tensions and stream of rushing thoughts in a young man's mind. He is very resourceful, charming, and organized—until he isn't, and things run out of his control.

Christos met "tough love." He was expelled. But the emphasis was on love. If he could get his act together, he could come back for his graduation year. And that kind of thing happened if a teacher or houseparent would vouch for the potential of a student.

You know, Notre Dame has had students who have gone on to win and coach Stanley Cups, represent Canada at championships, run their own businesses, become politicians, excel in education, law, engineering, the military, the corporate world, and space science—even climb Mount Everest. These are thrilling accomplishments for the college to witness. But this prodigal son narrative warms the heart as much. The goal of Athol Murray College of Notre Dame was met in this student—a self-reliant graduate who, under God, took the initiative to achieve, gave back to his community, and has remained loyal to the bonds formed at Notre Dame.

The road was circuitous.

Introduction

 t's been several years, but I can remember my surroundings clearly. After all, every Hound remembers their first time in Wilcox—their first rumble on the 4-Mile[4] road, loose gravel roughly massaging the undercarriage of the car as they ride into town. It's impossible to forget the large but dying grain elevator to your left that looks like it's going to collapse at any moment.[5]

Lane Hall, an old, decaying building, suffocates you with history as you turn north onto Main Street. Move forward ten meters, and across the street, you'll find an outdated, red-painted sign, signifying the only real store in town. The Hound Shop[6] sells snacks and other essentials to students and school apparel

1

mainly to visiting relatives of students attending the nearby Athol Murray College of Notre Dame.

Through the first intersection on Main Street, you'll find the trailer-style buildings that read Carr Hall and McCusker Hall. They sit across the street from one another like two hockey players lined up at faceoff, with letters screwed onto their wood signs. Rust rings have formed around them with age.

Take a few steps down the sidewalk, and you're at the church, its stained-glass windows grabbing your attention.

The dining hall, called Varsity, sits directly across the street from the church.

Further up from Varsity, you'll find two two-story buildings connected by a lounge area, or "link." These two structures, parallel to one another, are the dormitories known as Fred Hill and Max Bell, named after two predominant contributors to the college. Looking south from the link, you can still see the highway about 400 meters out. You can spot this building, the second largest on campus, within seconds of driving onto Wilcox's Main Street.

East of Fred Hill and Max Bell is Seaman Hall. During my time in Wilcox, Seaman was the newest building on campus, and the best way to describe it is as an oversized bungalow. Once on the inside, you might think it's a very well-kept frat house, as it's the temporary home to more than sixty male students.

While Fred Hill sits to the left of Seaman, the Mother Teresa dorm sits to the right. This is the girls' dorm. The mystery of what is going on in there still lurks in the mind of every adolescent male who passes. However, Notre Dame has strict rules: Don't go past the wooden sign with the dwelling's name; it is strictly off-limits for the boys.

Connecting the residential buildings are either sidewalks or a combination of gravel and concrete. All three buildings form together in perfect harmony, with the central core being Canada Park.[7]

A staple of Wilcox, Canada Park is home to grass benches and statues of the men who defined the school and spent a lifetime preserving it. Three flags blow in the wind twenty-five feet above the park with pride. The flags of Canada, Saskatchewan, and Notre Dame all stand equal to one another. It is through this area of campus that many students make their march to weekly classes and Sunday Mass.

This is not, however, the case for the youngest of students who are attending Notre Dame. Young boys, like myself at the time, start their Hound experience at Edith Hall.

Edith Hall basically sits between the church and the building that most Notre Dame Hounds remember most: Duncan Mac-Neil Arena. Getting closer to Edith Hall, you walk up a path of uneven bricks that look like they've been repositioned multiple times. I suppose their lack of uniformity adds character and acts as a symbol of what is to come.

The first wall of the building smacks your eyes with Chicago-style red bricks and periodic windows that go all the way around the building. Its triangle-shaped roof that greets you is in desperate need of new shingles. The roof is high and would come in handy for mischief down the road. I personally have not seen anything like it. I'm not sure who would design such a thing. Really, it is the black sheep of the structure, as this weird triangle looks nothing like the rest of the building.

The front room through the triangle opening is named the Marshall Center. To the left is a place we call the Fish Bowl, as it is practically a glass room. To the right is the dormitory's houseparents' room—purposely placed right next to the door to ensure any night-crawling students aren't able to make it outside.

Picture dozens of pre-teen boys entering this place for the first time, scared yet excited at the same time, all standing around, all complete strangers to one another.

Prologue

he day I got expelled from Athol Murray College of Notre Dame, which isn't really a college but a private school (like a prep school but without the uniforms), was the worst day of my life. I wasn't just leaving "ND." I was leaving my life behind. I had spent the last few years making a name for myself, and it had finally caught up to me. All my friends, the daily laughs and odd struggles, were gone. I was out. That was it. I wanted to be angry at somebody, but I couldn't because there was no one to blame but myself. I had created a shitstorm and now I was dry-heaving in it.

It was the last day of October 2004. I had a layover into Edmonton and called my sister, who was attending college at the time, from a payphone. She was at a Halloween party, but I told her that I had to see her, that it was urgent. She came. My sister's not an emotional person—I think we've hugged twice in our lives. We didn't hug this time, but when I told her that I got expelled and had to leave the school the next day, she started crying. That was the only time I ever saw my sister cry.

***

Back at school, I made the rounds and said my goodbyes. They went too fast, like a blur. I was lost. Gutted. Empty. Just numb. And there was no time left.

Then, I was in John's car and headed to the airport in Regina. I could have taken a taxi, but John had been my houseparent and rugby coach for three years, and he volunteered to take me. John was a great guy—a better friend than I deserved. He'd given up a professional coaching career to work at Notre Dame. He had attended the school himself as a teenager and came back to be a positive influence on kids like me.

"You can take a taxi, or I can drive you," he said. "What do you want to do?"

"I want you to take me," I replied. I like to think he was holding on like I was, not ready to say goodbye. Going with John gave me another forty-five minutes to feel like part of the school. Like a Hound.

At the airport, John asked me if I wanted to get dropped off or if I wanted him to come in. I did want him to come in with me, and I could tell he wanted to also. I thought he had some advice for me and was waiting for the right moment. I needed to hear something that would help me make sense of what had just happened. He must have something to tell me about the mess I had just made of my life.

Before going through security, we decided to get something to eat at Burger King in the airport's food court. "You know," said John, leaning in...

Here it comes, I thought, that wisdom that's going to make it all better. I needed to hear it. You have no idea how badly I needed it.

"The secret," he said, "to getting hot French fries is to order them without salt. Then they have to make a fresh batch. You can add the salt later yourself."

That was great advice, sure. Just horrible timing.

John walked me to the security gate, and I think I hugged him. I kind of blanked after that, to be honest. I don't remember what happened, but I remember how I felt. I'd been crying on and off for days. I cried when they told me I was expelled. I bawled my eyes out on the phone with my mom. Walking to the gate, entirely alone for the first time in years, I cried again, heading for the unknown. I wasn't a student anymore. I wasn't a Hound. Whatever lay at the other end of this flight would be completely different, and it wasn't going to be good.

On the plane, I settled into my seat and put my head down. I was still crying, but softly now, because I didn't want to bother anybody. I just couldn't stop. I tilted my ballcap over the top of my face and wept, doing my best to hold it in. My upper body was shaking. An older woman sitting next to me in the window seat put her hand on my back. "Young man," she said. "What's the matter?"

"My life," I said, "it's over." That's exactly how I felt. At seventeen, I'd screwed up so badly that there was no going back, no making things right.

"Oh no," she said, "I think it's just beginning!"

It would be years before I realized she was right. My life was just beginning.

People say there's always a light at the end of the tunnel, but what if there is no tunnel? Sometimes things get so bad that you can't see your way out. You know that no good will come out of a situation, and you're just kind of stuck there in limbo, waiting to see if it's going to get worse. I'm not talking about depression. It's more like total defeat.

People say other things too, like, "It's not about getting knocked down; it's about getting back up." Well, sometimes you can't even think about getting up because you can't breathe and you're still falling. That's how it was for me that day on the plane. Eventually, I stopped falling and got back on my feet. But before I could stand like a man, I had to face reality. I had to learn to take responsibility for my mistakes and accept the consequences.

I may have thought I was special, but I'm no more special than anybody else. We all have to deal with our own consciences, and no amount of denial, no pushing the blame on other people, makes that go away. You can tell people you're not malicious, not the bad guy. You can say you wouldn't hurt anybody, at least not intentionally. But none of that matters if you cross a line. This time, I crossed a line I couldn't get back from and there was no charming my way out of it. All I could do was face it, learn from it, and try to make up for it. Eventually, I had to figure out how to forgive myself.

Getting kicked out of high school may seem trivial to you. To a kid like me, at that time in my life, it was huge. But now I have some perspective, and I understand why I thought my life was over. I can also see how ridiculous that thinking was. But you don't see things that way when you're in the middle of them. You don't see anything—just the problems.

You might be going through a tough time right now. Maybe you're waiting for someone to show you the way. That's probably not going to happen. You have to show yourself the way. That light—it's in you. It's the good part inside you that's telling you what's right. But you can't see it if you're blaming other people. Your problems, whether you brought them on yourself or not, are yours to deal with.

I grew up in the small town of Fort McMurray, Alberta, Canada. My parents are both Greek. Mom was born to Greek parents in Halifax and Dad immigrated from a small village called *Mavrommati*, which means "black eye" in Greek. We were a typical Hellenic family, with a family-owned restaurant. My mom and dad had a pizza place. They really wanted to send me to a private school, but during their early years in the restaurant business, money was tight. My older brother started hanging with what my parents considered to be a "rough crowd." In hindsight, they weren't that bad. The kids smoked a little weed, but they weren't criminals. Okay, so some of them went to jail—maybe some are still in jail. Anyway, as I got older, Mom and Dad worried that I'd fall in with the same type of crowd, so even though it cost them a lot, they sent me to Notre Dame in the little town of Wilcox, in Saskatchewan.

Athol Murray College of Notre Dame is a big hockey school, and I don't even play hockey. Okay, I played. Badly. I mean, I was horrible. In my whole hockey career (if you could call it that), I never made even one complete stop, but it didn't matter because I couldn't skate either. I didn't even fully understand the uniform. When the guys told me the flaps on the helmet were to keep my ears warm, I believed them. Anyway, I don't think my parents sent me to ND thinking I'd be the next Wayne Gretzky. The school's also known for keeping kids on the straight and narrow, so that probably had something to do with their decision.

At first, I didn't want to go. I didn't want to leave my Fort Mc-Murray friends behind. I cried when I left for Notre Dame, and I cried again when I got kicked out. A lot can happen in a few years. Those years were the most pivotal time in my life. It's a time that will stick with me till I die. The people of ND—the teachers, the houseparents, the administration, and especially the students—made me who I am today.

I'm not a psychologist. I'm not a therapist, a counselor, or a coach—just a regular kid who made mistakes and went through a tough time. I can't give you any professional advice, but I can tell you my personal story, and maybe you can see yourself in it.

I didn't really understand what that lady on the plane was trying to tell me until years later, but it gave me the hope I needed to keep moving forward. To see what was waiting for me on the other side.

This book is about the choices I made that got me kicked out of school. Putting them down on paper is my way of owning them. I hope they teach you something about life, and make you laugh, or help you deal with your bad choices. Because no matter where you are in life, no matter how much you screwed up, your life isn't over. It's just beginning. I hope people high up in private planes and down in remote villages can feel as if they're right beside me as I relive my past in the stories in this book.

Some of the staff at Notre Dame (the ones left from my time there) still talk about what happened—among themselves and sometimes to students. I've visited the school since then, and when I introduce myself, I often get curious looks...or I get asked if I'm the guy they learned about who did this or that when I was a student there. I started writing this book because so many times they got the stories wrong, saying I did things that I didn't do and leaving out the parts that actually happened. I wanted to set the record straight.

Those who were there have called what happened "the greatest story ever told." Some say it's a legend. But there's only one person who can tell you how it all went down, so I'd like to do that. Even though no one's asked my opinion about what happened, I'll tell you right now what I think: it was very stupid. But let's get on with it. Then you can decide. Here we go...

Chapter 1

Rodeo Day

inth grade starts out with all the parents at the school. Not much happens these first days. The teachers have already picked our roommates for us, and now we get our schedules—that sort of stuff. Notre Dame's hockey team is called the "Hounds," and the students and alumni refer to themselves as Hounds too. Depending on your house color, you're either a Badger, a Chopper, a Marauder, or a Gunner. My house is blue, and I'm a Gunner.

A few days into the school year is Rodeo Day. We all meet in Varsity, which is the assembly hall and the cafeteria. The staff takes turns explaining Rodeo Day (which sounds kind of like a track meet or a field day) and how we need to work together and support each other to win points for our houses. There's some friendly banter among some of the students and teachers who've done this before, and that makes it sound like fun. A lot of the older students are wearing face paint, wild hats, and crazy-looking clothes, and they're carrying props that make it look like they're prepared for the battlefield. The rest of us are just in our house colors, supposedly so we can tell each other apart out there. Badgers are orange, Choppers are green, Marauders are maroon, and then there's the Gunners like me, in blue. I'm getting pretty fired up, I am honored to be a Gunner and I haven't even done anything yet, but all this talk makes me feel proud to be wearing blue and calling myself a Gunner.

We head outside to the football field[8] for relay races, potato sack races, and other games. Every student is on the field, about 300 of us from all grades. So there's all these kids, our parents are gone, and then there's the staff, which is way outnumbered by the students. I'm feeling a little uneasy and kind of vulnerable around all these older kids. That's when I realize the races are just a side attraction. The main event of Rodeo Day is the most ridiculous thing I've ever seen in all my fifteen years.

There's a white line, like a box, that runs around the interior of the field, and everyone's lined up around it. It's a solid wall of students standing shoulder-to-shoulder, so you can't see what's going on behind them. The kids across the field from me are wearing different colored shirts than mine and they're staring me down, like they're angry or something. I look away because I don't want to make eye contact with these guys or even the girls. I'm just a fifteen-year-old pudgy Greek kid with glasses. These kids can smell fear, and right now, I'm stinking of it. I'm terrified.

A teacher approaches me and asks if I'm having a good time. I hide my fear and tell her, "Yeah, this is so much fun." I should say, "for the love of God get me out of here," but I don't want to seem weak or scared. I'm a high schooler now, and I want to be a man. No more Mom and Dad. I'm on my own, and it's time to get tough. But first I'm positive I'm going to get my ass kicked.

A loud bang goes off. It's the starting gun for a hundred-meter dash in the middle of the field. It's also the perfect distraction for what's about to go down. The school staff is focused on the race, and they don't see what's happening beyond the wall of students.

Now the kids on the other side of the field are pointing at me. They break up like a pack of wolves, three to the left and three to the right. I want to hide, to blend in, but there's nowhere to go. This is a far cry from the complimentary brochure I got in the mail before my parents enrolled me in the school, the one with photos of all those nice kids and smiling faces.

They're on me. I try to take my shirt off to surrender, but a hand grabs my face and pulls my shirt down so I can't. I realize they're not after my colors—they want the blood of a Greek virgin. They want to put me in a human washing machine full of fists. They're screaming at me, punching me, kicking me, and slapping me, and it hurts all over. Across the field I see another kid getting beat on. They take all his clothes—even his shoes. He's standing in his boxers, pink all over, while the other students laugh.

All the ninth-graders—the "new boys"—are getting their tails beat in, and I realize we're the only ones who didn't see it coming. They do this every year, so all the older kids were waiting for it over the summer. Waiting for their chance to make up for the beating they took as new boys. No one's helping us, not even the older kids in our same colors. The staff is still running the races in the middle of the field, and my senior "allies"—the older Gunners—are looking for ninth-grade Badgers, Choppers, and Marauders to beat on. They don't even make eye contact with me.

This goes on forever, and it's not just guys. The girls are involved too. Big guys ripping clothes off small guys. Girls ripping at each other. It's insane. I saw that movie *Braveheart* one time, and I feel like I'm in it. Just mayhem. There's ripped-up clothes all over the field and some kids tear off strips and make them into headbands and bandanas.

There's a lull and some guys are circling me like they're stalking prey or something. I'm standing there half-naked and embarrassed, so I find a random maroon-colored shirt on the ground and I stick my hands in it. I get my arms through it, but before I can get my head in, two guys grab me from behind and yank me off my feet. Now I'm hanging off my shirt like it's a clothesline and they're dragging me down the field. I'm terrified. I turn my head to look at these guys and I recognize them from my hometown. They have blue shirts on, so why are they attacking me?

"I'm a Gunner! I'm a Gunner!" I'm yelling in my high-pitched, choir boy voice. They drop me, and one guy says, "What are you, nuts? You don't put on another color, you idiot!" I sarcastically tell them I don't know the rules. And now I have a rug burn from my left ear all across the back of my neck to my right shoulder and it hurts.

Between being knocked around, I can see the races are still going. In the middle of the field, there's sled races where they put a small kid in a thing like a dog sled and a big kid puts on a harness and drags the sled with the kid in it to the finish line.

We're out there for a couple of hours, and then it's time to go inside, so I get with the other Gunners and keep my head down. *Is this it? Is this the end, or is something else going to happen?* I don't know what to expect, but I'm scared. We're in the Marshall Center, where my dorm is, and there's kids bleeding and crying.

There's kids with purple nipples and bite marks. Some of them have ice packs and some are getting bandaged up. I didn't get it the worst.

I'm hoping Rodeo Day is just one day, because I don't know if I can do a week of this, let alone a whole year.

Chapter 2

He's Having a Seizure

I'm one month into my first year, and I see how it works here at Notre Dame. You really have to look out for yourself. We live in cubicles in the dorm rooms, which is just like a cube in an office with four sides and no top or bottom. One wall, which is part of the building, is cinder blocks, and the other walls are made of laminated wood. There's six cubes in a row on one wall and six on the other, with an aisle in between and a study area at the end. The cubes are old, but there's a swinging door so you have some privacy. Each cubicle has cupboards, a locker, and a bed.

Someone left a dirty magazine in my cubicle, and I'm looking at it when this house leader, Patrick Glass, walks in. House leaders are older students who are supposed to keep the younger ones in line. If you want to go to college after Notre Dame, it looks good on your college application, like you had a leadership role at the school. Mostly the house leaders use it as an excuse to make life miserable for new boys like me. Patrick has this grin on his face, and I can see where this is going. The whole thing's probably a set-up. I'm frantic, trying to block the door so he can't leave my cube. If he gets away, he's going to get me in trouble and I know it. I need to stop him and explain to him how this isn't even my magazine. I don't know where it came from.

Patrick towers over me. He's older, fitter, and a lot stronger. I don't stand a chance. My best bet is to just get away at this point. I squirm past him, but I don't get far, and we end up in the hallway. He's wrestling me for the magazine, and I can't let him have it because that's going to get me in all kinds of trouble. But he's bigger than me and now he's got me pinned. I'm standing up against the chalkboard that's hanging on the cinder block wall in the study area. He starts shaking me, and I bang my head against the chalkboard. That's when it clicks with me: *this is my chance to get out of this.* I slump to the ground like a wet noodle. It's the only way I can think of to get out of this mess. I'm just fifteen years old, and if I let the older kids push me around, it's going to be a very long year.

A few kids laugh, thinking it's a joke. Patrick gives me a few light kicks, but I just lie there like I'm knocked out. "Hey man," he says, "get up." But I don't move. I'm in full character now. This is some of my best work, I'm thinking, and all I have to do is lie here. I keep my eyes closed but I can hear people gathering around. "Get up, man," somebody else says. More laughs. Still, I don't move.

This is all happening by the stairs right outside Marcy's door. She's the houseparent for our dorm. Then I hear Marcy's voice.

"What's happening?" she says. I can hear her footsteps coming toward me. Everybody gets quiet, and I guess this is serious now. I want to open my eyes, but that would ruin it, so I have to depend on my ears, which is kind of ironic because I've never been a good listener. Right now, I'm listening hard. Like it's Christmas Eve and Santa may be on the roof.

More kids are gathering around—their voices frantic. "Christos, wake up! Wake up!" The hallway is filling up and the tone has shifted. Nobody's laughing. Marcy must have gone for help because there's an older guy leaning over me. I can smell his breath. He grabs my shoulders.

"Christos," he says, and gives me a light shake. Then, "Let's get him on his back." I moan for effect and roll onto my side. The guy's checking my pulse and a woman's hand is on my forehead, I guess checking my temperature or something.

"Call an ambulance," she yells. These people must be from the healthcare center, the school's infirmary. Time to step it up a notch. I start harvesting spit in my mouth and let it run out. I can feel it dribbling down my face. Kind of gross, but it does the trick.

"He's having a seizure!" somebody screams.

I can't believe how well this is all working out.

"Paramedics are on the way," somebody says, and I realize maybe this went a little too far. It's too late now, though. I can't just jump up and yell, "Gotcha!"

"Get Christian," I breathe weakly. He's my best friend from back home in Fort McMurray, and probably the reason my parents sent me to Notre Dame in the first place. They figured we'd keep each other company or something. Anyway, Regina General Hospital is forty-five minutes away, and since I'm calling the shots now, I'm going to want company for the ambulance ride. After a few more feeble cries for my friend, he's by my side. His mouth is almost touching my ear and he whispers, "I know you're faking, you son of a bitch."

I'm about to burst, but I hold it in. Christian knows me better than anybody and knows it's all a sham. He's probably thinking the same thing as me right now too: that getting busted for a dirty magazine isn't anywhere near as bad as what I'm pulling right now. I have to see it through.

I hear two new voices and it's the medics. One's talking to me and the other one's relaying the terms of protocol, the whole procedure—whatever it is. I don't know what's coming next, but I just have to go with it for now. I can hear the beeps of medical equipment and I blink fast and catch a glimpse of a stretcher. *Pull back the curtains—it's show time.* They count to three and lift me up and I'm on the stretcher. My eyes are closed, but I sense a lot of eyes on me. I'm elevated and moving, and I can feel a cool breeze blowing across my body. An hour has passed since I started this charade and it's nice to be outside in the fresh air after lying on the floor. Even this play gets an intermission. They're sliding me into the ambulance and I figure it's time to wake up. I blink my eyes.

"Wow, how did I get here?" I say. I hope my fake surprise voice is good enough.

I wave my arms like a child having a tantrum, and one of the paramedics says, "Let's drop him," and they strap me in and fasten the buckles. I say I'm cold and they cover me with a blanket.

I unbuckle the top strap, then the second strap, and the paramedic refastens them. I unbuckle them again, and fake passing out. The paramedic buckles them, and we're playing this game of buckling of unbuckling as I pretend to go in and out of consciousness.

It's comical, I think, until one of the paramedics, a woman, says, "You need to stay awake or we're going to have to put a needle in you." She isn't joking, and I open my eyes wide, opting to stay awake for the ride.

Regina's the capital of Saskatchewan, and it's a stark contrast from Wilcox, which is in the middle of nowhere. They wheel me into a hospital room and I fake being unconscious again. I have no clue what they're doing—giving me all kinds of tests and trying to figure out what's wrong with me, I guess. They won't find anything. This goes on for an hour and the doctor sits me up. I act like I'm slowly coming to. Christian's there, and Marcy, along with some doctors. They all drove out together, and they're going to drive me back. The doctor gives some instructions to the adults and we all leave.

Christian and I are in the back seat and I'm holding an ice pack against the back of my head. We look at each other and grin, then turn away so we don't burst out laughing. Back at campus, my room's all tidy. Somebody even made the bed and there's two pillows. One of the guys comes in my cubicle and says, "Man,

Patrick thought he really hurt you. He was crying. He felt so bad, he cleaned your room for you."

I lay down, put my hands behind my head, and grin like I just stole Christmas from everyone in Whoville.

Mission accomplished.

Chapter 3

Jell-O

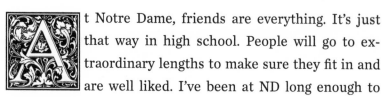

At Notre Dame, friends are everything. It's just that way in high school. People will go to extraordinary lengths to make sure they fit in and are well liked. I've been at ND long enough to make friends with other new boys, but I'm craving some acknowledgment and respect from the older guys, at least the tenth-graders. They have it all. Once you've been here a year, you can go to the front of the line in the cafeteria and nobody calls you out. Nobody gets in your face about every little thing.

I'm sitting at a table here in Varsity, which is a fancy name for the dining hall, surrounded by a bunch of other goofy grade-nine boys. We're talking amongst ourselves when out of the corner of my eye I see this girl heading toward the table in front of ours. She's an older student and she looks pissed. She's got her hair tied back and an angry look on her face. On the far side of the room, all the girls have their eyes glued on this one girl, like they know what she's up to. *What is she doing?* Carrying a drink or something. She walks past a few people at the table, all older kids, stops in front of this guy, and dumps the whole cup—it looks like water—right in his lap.

"You're an asshole," she says. Then she turns on her heel and walks back to the other side of the room, where the girls are clapping, howling, and whistling. The boys at the guy's table are making deep-pitched sounds—*ooo* and *wooooow*. On the other side of the room, the girls have their hands up to high-five the girl as she passes.

What just happened?

This guy that she dumped the water on is one of the real popular kids. He's sitting there in his soaked shirt and pants and his friends are all staring at him. I'm staring too. Nobody knows how to react.

Then he says, "Somebody needs to teach that witch a lesson." I don't even think. In a split second, I'm on my feet and my mouth's open.

"I'll do it!" I squeal. Everybody at our table and the other one is looking at me now.

The dude, Jason, says, "And what are you gonna do, you little weasel?"

I'm standing there like a pylon, and I know what they're all thinking: *What is this pudgy little nobody going to do?* I look around, frantically searching for an idea. *This is my chance to be somebody.*

I blurt out, in my embarrassingly high-pitched, fifteen-year-old whine, "I'll throw a pudding at her!"

"No," he says, pointing straight at me. "You'll throw it in her face." Jason leans back in his chair. He smirks and nods at the guys around the table, like he's pleased with himself.

They're all going to know who I am when this is over. They're all going to chant my name.

Jason's table and mine are buzzing. He calls me over and I make my way to his table. I can't see anything but his face—the rest of the room has gone fuzzy—and I'm focused on getting over there without falling on my face. I crouch down next to him, and we huddle together. He gives me instructions: *the best place to do it is outside of Varsity.* I'm supposed to wait until she goes to get her backpack.

We all have to leave our backpacks on the ground outside the door before entering Varsity. Don't ask me why—we just do. Then we pick them back up on the way out.

Jason says, "Hurry up, man, before she gets done eating." He wants this done today. Now.

Yes, oh great and popular one that I admire.

I head over to the dessert display, which is basically just a long table, like a cart on wheels that you'd see in a hospital cafeteria. Or a gymnasium. It's no Willy Wonka and the Chocolate Factory, but it's all we have. There's all these sweets laid out, and I grab a Jell-O pudding. It's light-colored, not sure what kind, and I poke my finger in the plastic container ever so gently. *Mmm... banana cream.* I hold it down by my side, head outside, and wait for the signal. Jason runs out with a pudding in his hand and hides around the corner of the building. I don't know what's going on—this wasn't discussed and there's no time to find out now—so I stick to the plan. I get the signal and here comes a bunch of girls. I spot her in the group and watch her bend down to get her backpack. I run up to her.

"Hey!" I yell, so she'll look up at me, which she does—like I'm a wild animal at the zoo. I pitch the cup of pudding at her so hard, the plastic shatters across her face. In those split seconds, I smell the creamy banana goodness in the air. She's in shock, and before she can even react, *wham*—here comes Jason from behind the building. He grabs her backpack and dumps his pudding in it. Then he gets in her face, mouth open, tongue hanging out, shaking his head back and forth like a gargoyle.

He's shouting at her, "How do you like that? Huh?" She's bawling now, I can tell by the way her body's shaking and the sounds she's making, but I can't see the tears because of all the pudding gooped all over her entire face. It was a direct hit.

Someone grabs my arm—a teacher. I twist out of her grip and make a run for it. Fred Hill is a dormitory for tenth- and eleventh-graders, and I've never gone in there before, but I run straight for the place. The guys are laughing and hollering, and they clap for me and slap me on the back, and it feels great. I mean, it's amazing.

I find Jason, and he wants to know if I said anything to the teacher that grabbed me. He really just wants to know if I snitched on him.

"No," I tell him, "I didn't say anything." We're surrounded now and everyone's looking at me. I know how it works by now. I understand the hierarchy. I'm prepared for the consequences of what I did, but I wouldn't survive the consequences of snitching on a fellow schoolmate.

Jason grabs me by the front of my shirt, and he's got me up against the concrete wall. He's looking me dead in the eye and I start mumbling like a fool.

"Nothing," I say. "I didn't say anything. I wouldn't. Not ever." He doesn't say a word, doesn't have to. I know that if I snitch, I'm a dead man.

I also know I'm still in for a massive amount of trouble. I stay away from Varsity for the rest of my lunch hour and it's killing me, wondering what's going to happen. But there's some good news. Faith Peters was the first staff member to get to the girl and she took her to the healthcare center. Faith is my homeroom teacher and she knows me. She's also married to the principal, Owen. Maybe she'll take pity on me, one of the new boys under pressure to fit in. I sure hope so.

The lunch bell rings and I'm walking to homeroom. I can see Faith standing at the far end of the hallway as people scatter and get ready for classes to resume. We lock eyes from about thirty feet away. She's pissed. Her face looks all tight and her lips are pressed together in a line. She waves her hand slowly, motioning me over. I know that look. My mom gives me that look all the time.

"Follow me," she says. Faith takes me to the back of McCusker Hall, where there's a staff lounge area with some chairs and a couple of offices. I've seen kids get disciplined here before. She directs me to one of the offices and tells me to sit. I brace for the worst.

The funny thing is, Faith isn't yelling. Her voice is soft and sweet, almost pleasant. But firm, too, like she's scolding a little puppy that peed on the floor.

"I know someone put you up to this, Christos," she says in a motherly voice. "But you should have a mind of your own." Faith goes on and on about the school being a place where young men build character and decide who they want to be. She says that I'm at a point in my life where I should be making decisions about the kind of man I want to become.

I can't believe how this is going down. No lecture? No punishment? I just smashed a pudding cup in a girl's face and all I get is a motivational speech? I can't believe my luck.

Faith's asking me about thinking for myself and being my own man. All that stuff. I keep my answers short: "Yeah, I know." "Of course." "You're right."

I leave the room knowing I've done something horrible, yet I don't even feel bad about it. I feel good—like I just won a battle. Wars, I think, have been fought for independence, glory, and resources. Wars have casualties. Lucky for me, the only casualty I have to deal with, Faith, isn't even all that upset with me. Everything else can be fixed with a nice hot shower. Like they say, "the juice is worth the squeeze." This time, the pudding was worth the toss and the aftermath speaks for itself.

Now I'm getting nods from upperclassmen. I'm inching my way to the top of the food chain around here.

Chapter 4

LockDown

It's midwinter, and our dorm is in shit yet again. It seems getting in trouble is second nature by now—like breathing for my friends and me. Marcy has us on lockdown, which means we can't leave our dorm room. So, it's seven other guys and me with eight cubicles, a study area, and a couple of bathrooms. And locked doors at either end.

Lockdown at school never feels like punishment to me. When my parents sent me to my room, that was punishment. But when you're stuck with six of your best friends plus one guy you like to pick on, it's not so bad. We give Greg a hard time because he's a scrawny kid and an easy target. Sure, that's no reason to single a guy out, but there isn't much else to do. We're just hanging around the study area, bored as hell. It must have occurred to Greg that if we don't figure out a way to amuse ourselves quick, we're going to start in on him.

So he pipes up, "Hey guys, we should have a water fight."

A water fight. It's brilliant. We don't have much in that dorm, but with two bathroom stalls and two shower stalls, we have plenty of water. Everybody grabs mop buckets, cups, even garbage cans. One guy changes into his swim trunks and we all do the same. We don't think about what all that water is going to do to the walls, or the beds, or the carpeting. But we're getting wet—soaked to the skin—and we want to be comfortable.

We start slinging water around, splashing it all over the dorm and each other. Man, it's so much fun, screaming and laughing and whooping it up. Even Greg's laughing, throwing water at everybody. Pretty soon, guys from the other dorms hear us and they're trying to get in, but they can't because Marcy locked the door from the outside with the master key. These other guys can see us through the window in the door, though, and they start banging on that door as hard as they can, slamming into it and hollering at us to let them in. They can't believe what's going on in this room. We're kind of putting on a show for them too because the only thing better than a water fight is a water fight with an audience that wants to join in and can't.

Of course, Marcy hears all that racket and pretty soon she shows up. We can see her sourpuss face in the window, and she's pissed. She holds up the master key and gives us that look, like, "Fun's over, boys, and you are all gonna pay for this." We see her going for the lock. If she gets in the room, the water fight's over. But that door doesn't swing out into the hallway—it swings *into* the room. So we jam our feet against the bottom and she can't get in. Now she's really pissed, and she scowls at us through the window, and one of the guys takes a bucket of water and throws it against the glass. We can see the water dripping down the window pane and it looks as if water was thrown in her face. This gets us just roaring.

Now, lockdown is one of the worst punishments you can get. I mean not to me, but it's one of the worst punishments the school hands out. And here we are, making it the best entertainment a guy can have. We don't want it to end. Marcy's out there for an hour, maybe longer. By now, everyone else out there has gone back to their rooms. They know we're in deep shit, and they don't want any part of it. After a while, we're just worn out. The carpet's soaked through—everything's soaked through. There's puddles. So we let up, and we let her in.

We have to clean up that mess, of course. Hours and hours with the steam cleaner, sucking dirty water out of the carpet. Countless trips to the washroom to empty the dirty water. Even then, we're laughing the whole time.

Later, there's punishment—workouts, which are like bootcamp. They're usually outside, and they're brutal. Forty-five minutes, an hour of high-intensity pushups, sit-ups, sprints...basically pushing us to exhaustion. This time, it's workouts till we're sore and ready to drop.

I'll never regret what we did. None of us will. I think we all kind of realized the worst thing the administration can do is lock us in a room together, but it's up to us to decide whether it's punishment or fun. They don't own us. We own us.

I think that was kind of a breaking point for Marcy. She looks at us differently now. We aren't Hounds to her; we're wild dogs that she can't handle. Ultimately, *we* have control.

Chapter 5

The Hole

 aturday starts out the same as every other week-end. Sleep in as late as we want. Well, for me, anyway, because I don't play sports. Eat breakfast. Then the day is ours.

The Marshall Center has a lounge on the main floor at the end of the hall. It's a big room with carpeting and an old twenty-seven-inch cube TV complete with fake wood laminate. There's a payphone and soda machine on the left side of the lounge. On the right side is this door. There's a room back there for storage and old junk. Leftover hockey equipment and other stuff that nobody uses, but nobody wants to throw away either. The door's always locked and nobody thinks about it much. None of us has ever stepped foot in that room. We just catch glimpses when houseparents and teachers go inside.

Today, for some reason, the door's open. Not all the way, just a crack. Enough to make you want to swing it open and see what's in there. There's maybe half a dozen guys in the lounge, and we're all eyeing that door. There's no houseparents around, and I have to take a look. I have to.

I'm standing there next to Lou, a dark-haired, soft-spoken guy.

"Let's take a peek," I say. "I'll watch the door and you go in." The door between the hallway and the lounge has a window made of diamond-shaped red and yellow panes of glass. It's the wavy kind, like in church, so you can't see through it too well, just shadows on the other side. I train my eyes on the wavy glass. I won't know who's coming, but I'll see their silhouette through the red and yellow diamonds.

Lou opens the door to the storeroom ever so slowly and steps inside. He's practically swallowed up by all the junk. It's really crammed in there. One of the guys gets the idea to pack everything against the walls, then he starts packing everything that's in the lounge into that room. The usual mischief. That sounds good, and Skip, this skinny kid whose dad is a fisherman, says we need a broom. I get him to cover the door and I get a broom, and he starts sweeping like crazy. There's dust flying everywhere and I'm trying not to gag. I'm not really watching the door anymore—I'm watching Skip. He stops sweeping and his eyes get real wide.

"There's something here."

Skip drops the broom and leans over the floor, and now I see it. There's a square of laminate that blends in with the rest of the floor, but it's not a perfect match. Skip tries to lift the edge, but it doesn't budge. Lou gets this grin on his face and lifts an index finger. He looks around at us and says, "Let's put everything back...for now."

We do like he says, putting everything just the way it was and leaving the door open a tiny crack. Everybody's smiling like girls at the spring dance and my imagination's running wild. What could possibly be under that hundred-year-old square of floor? We'll be back, with the right tools.

We all head back to our dorms for forks, spoons, knives—anything we can use to pry up that floorboard. At lunch, we grab more. You're not supposed to borrow anything from Varsity, so we sneak it out in our pockets. Back at the Marshall Center, there's no one around. Perfect. We throw caution to the wind and nobody guards the door. Everybody crouches on the floor and we start with the knives, prying at the edges of the dirty laminate. Then the pane glass door that nobody's watching opens and we all look up. I'm holding my breath, but it's just Frenchie. We call him that because he's from Quebec. He reminds everybody of Moose from the Archie comics, but we don't call him that to his face.

"What are you guys doing?" he says.

Lou points and says, "Guard the door."

"Okay," says Frenchie. That's how things work around here. No one questions each other. We just get things done.

Now that we have a lookout, we can get back to business. The floorboard finally pops. It's laminate and particleboard. Underneath, there's nothing. A hole.

I'm thinking, *How far does it go? Is there a body down there?*

"Get me a flashlight," says Lou. We all know Lou's fearless, but this is nuts. "I'll get it," I say.

I go back to my dorm and check the cubes. Abs is there, this lanky kid from Calgary. He's dark-skinned, intelligent, and defiant to authority. He's been my partner in crime all through ninth grade.

"Gimme your flashlight," I say. He doesn't even ask why, just gets it out of a cupboard. I wave my hand, signaling him to follow me and he does, flashlight in hand. We walk through the lounge and into the storeroom, and Lou's standing inside the hole. He's got his shirt tied around the lower part of his face to keep the dust and dirt out of his nose and mouth. Abs hands him the flashlight and Lou disappears.

He's not in there five seconds and everybody's bombarding him with questions like reporters at a press conference.

"Just wait, for Chrissake!" he says. He's tossing stuff out of the hole and it's landing on the dirty floor. Coca-Cola bottles that must be forty years old. Milk caps, newspaper clippings, gun shells. Nothing too crazy. Lou comes out and tells us it's safe. Well, as safe as crawling underneath an old building with zero protection can be. We stumble over each other to be the next one in—we all want to see this hidden world under the storeroom.

Skip's the first one in, and I'm right after him. It's a crawl space, a dirt tunnel so small we're on our hands and knees. I press my hands against the walls and it gives. It's not hard and rocky, just soft earth. Lou hollers for us to get out—we'll come back later when there's more time to investigate. We get out of there and put everything back the way we found it. Lou grabs all the tools, plus the stuff he pulled out of the hole. You would never know we were in there, the way we leave it. But we leave that door open a tiny crack.

I'm in my room now, the cubes, and everyone's talking about the hole. So now almost everybody knows about it. They all have these theories about that tunnel, and some are so funny and absurd. You can't help but laugh. Even going to bed, we're still talking about it. *What's that tunnel for, and what else is in that hole?*

***

It's Sunday morning, and I'm up early. I head into the lounge and slump onto the old beige sofa in there. The door to the storeroom is closed again. There's a few boys playing cards, Frenchie, Cory, and some other guys. Mass isn't for a few hours, so we're just passing the time, telling jokes and goofing around.

Cory says, "What the hell was that noise?"

Huh, what noise? We tell him to shut up and get back to the card game. Then we hear something, like a weird mumbling noise coming from the vents or the walls. Frenchie gets up and puts his ear against one of the warm vents. Then he puts his hands around his mouth.

"Who's there?" he says in his broken English accent. I hear somebody, but I can't make out what they're saying. Now everybody's up, with their ears pressed up against the vents on both sides of the room. They're shouting at the mystery man in the wall. As usual, I run out of patience. I'm knocking on the storeroom.

"Open the door, open the goddamn door!" I'm yelling. The door swings open and it's Lou.

"Jesus," he says, "What took you guys so long?" He tells us he's been down there for hours, digging away.

"It goes all the way back to the end of the building and probably outside the wall."

Oh boy. Lou's been digging and digging and this thing goes back about seventy-five feet so far. It's like an escape tunnel out of the dorm.

After church and then lunch, we get to work. Lou and Frenchie are in the hole digging. They never went to church—they've been digging the whole time. I go outside and figure out where they are. Me and some other guys are digging up the dirt out there. We're using everything. Knives, spoons, our hands, even our shoes. I can hear Lou under the dirt—we're so close. Oh my gosh, I touch his fingers.

Lou wants us to be quiet, but I can't hold it in. I'm just too excited. This is the solution to all of my problems. A secret escape route. No more curfews. No more restless nights wishing I was someplace else. Boys are coming around from all over and they surround our little group. Everybody's being so loud, so I'm not surprised when Sturz, the stocky houseparent with slicked-back hair comes out the back door. Sturz is a good guy, until you piss him off. Then he's one mean mother. I can hear him already, pushing his way into the crowd and looking down at the hole.

"Jesus Christ, what did you weasels do?" he says, rubbing his leathery face and squinting like he's trying to figure it out. Then his head shoots up and his face is bright red.

"You dug a hole!" We quickly kick dirt over the hole, but it's too late. Sturz has to report us and put all this in his logbook. That way, whoever comes on duty after him knows who's in trouble.

We're supposed to have a dorm meeting every week, but lately, it's been almost twice a day and today we're definitely having one. No one's getting off either, because it's like the army where if one person's in trouble, you're all in trouble. It's Marcy on duty now and she wants answers.

There's nothing left to tell, though. The door was left open. We dug a hole. End of story. So we get our punishment. Marcy tells us to dress for outdoor workouts and after we bundle up, she makes us do indoor workouts with the heat blasting. We line up against the wall in the Marshall Center and do wall-sits, which is like a partial squat where you flex your quads, hamstrings, and calves to stay up against the wall until you feel like your legs are going to burst. We do sit-ups and pushups too, till our bodies ache and our arms burn and we go numb. In that heat, we're sweating like pigs. It's brutal, but we deserve it.

***

The next day, my arms are so sore that I can't even lift the shampoo bottle in the shower. I can barely get dressed. I drag my body down the hall and I can hear murmurs and moans from all the other guys too. I'm supposed to be headed to Varsity for breakfast, but I have to look. I'm in the Marshall Center, and I walk down that hallway and through the door with the red and yellow wavy paned glass. Sure enough, the door to the storeroom is shut and locked. I smirk to myself and walk back outside toward Varsity. Sure, we got caught. And we paid for it. But now we know what's behind that door. I bet they never leave it open again.

Chapter 6

The Grad Prank

 mpressive" is the best word I can think of to describe what happened today. Maybe add in "grand" or "marvelous," or "world-class."

Every year the graduating class leaves their mark on the school. That's the rumor anyway, but I'd never seen it with my own eyes. I'm still a first-year, a new boy. So this was the first time I witnessed what's known as the "grad prank."

Speaking from experience, pulling off a prank with even half a dozen guys can get complicated. No one can mess up, and no one can blab. They have to keep it a secret. But for this prank, there's all these people. Guys, girls, house leaders, hockey captains, students whose parents teach at the school. Every senior student is involved in the planning.

I heard about other pranks that graduating classes had pulled over the years, like hall slides, door slams, and leaners—harmless pranks that cause a little disruption. So I didn't expect much. But even those kinds of pranks can get complex. This year's graduating class is a big one. With so many people, I didn't expect the grad prank to go smoothly or even work. I still don't know how they pulled off the most complex mission in the history of grad pranks.

So this morning, I'm walking out of my dorm and I come around the brick wall to McCusker Hall. The sun hits those windows in the morning and it's so bright I never look that way, but I see a lot of kids staring up at those windows, so of course, I look. The reflection of the sun is so bright and it's right in my eyes, it nearly throws me off balance. I put my hand over my eyebrows to block the light and I can't believe what I see. The roof of Mc-Cusker Hall looks like a classroom. It looks like all the classrooms, because the graduating class took all the desks, chairs, and everything else out of the building and set them up there on the roof.

I keep walking, because I'm going to Varsity for breakfast, and there's a crowd gathering now. I'm standing behind all these backpacks and hoodies, staring up at that roof.

"Holy shit," people are saying. "How'd they get that up there?"

But there's more. I keep walking, past the church, and other classrooms are set up outside on the grass and in the street. I look down Main Street, and it's all classrooms. There's teachers' desks, students' desks, and everything else that wasn't nailed down right in the road. The graduating class has turned the Notre Dame campus inside out. Literally.

Kids are pouring out of the dorms now, and everyone's just gawking. The twelfth-graders are high-fiving. It's quite a display. This isn't a prank. It's artwork. As the day passes, I can see their handiwork everywhere. "Class of 2002" is scrawled on chalkboards, in books, and on the walls. The ice rink, now drained for the year, is piled high with desks, chairs, and tables like a giant Jenga puzzle ready to topple.

Muddling around campus with my friends, it's kind of funny watching all the adults try to deal with it. Nobody knows where to start or how to restore order. Eventually, they get us all to pitch in and clean it up. I'll take hauling desks and chairs over sitting in them to learn any day. Not only did the grad class put on a magnificent display for the entire school, but these fine scholars also helped me burn a whole school day.

I'm up in Kenny Hall, looking out the window at Duncan Mc-Neil Arena and the gymnasium. They must have done it last, because it's a complete cluster. Like they just threw everything in the middle of the gym and didn't even bother setting it up.

When I first saw McCusker Hall in the morning, I thought it was mostly the townies that did it, the students who live in town. But it wasn't. Everyone was involved—had to be, looking at the magnitude of this once-in-a-lifetime event—sixty, maybe seventy students. Somebody must have gotten a master key off a staff member. That's the only way they would have access to all the buildings and all the rooms. They came out in the middle of the night to do the deed. I can't imagine organizing all those people to get it done. That's a lot of hands, and they pulled it off. They must have been planning for weeks.

Nobody ever did anything like this before, and I bet no one ever does it again either. And that's why I tip my hat to the Class of 2002.

Chapter 7

The Ultimate Hall Slide

 ost of us are in the dorms on Sundays for "dorm room general," which means general cleaning for inspection. It also means generals like in the military, because that's what the houseparents act like when they inspect our rooms. If you don't pass the three dust wipe rule, you have to run a workout the next morning, which is a Monday, usually around six o'clock. Nobody wants to start the week with a workout.

You have to understand that these rooms are old, and they attract dust no matter how hard we clean. And since our house leaders don't like us, we almost always fail inspection. Rarely do they ever swipe around our room and not get dust on three of their fingers. Dorm room general usually takes two or three hours. We have to clean our cubes, the study room, and the bathrooms. It's getting near the end of the school year, and today, I'm not really interested in cleaning. Neither is anybody else.

Now, Edith Hall, our dorm building, has two main hallways that meet to form an "L." The floors are long, smooth stretches of tile with no breaks. They connect our dorm rooms where we have our cubicles and beds. Each bed is made up of two foam mattresses covered in light blue vinyl. It's smooth and slippery—the perfect texture for sliding.

Being the creative young adolescents that we are, we figure out that if we all flip our beds and lay the mattresses end to end down the hallway, we have a giant runway. Then we can ride another mattress down that long line of mattresses. So we make a game of it, taking turns to see who can get their mattress the farthest. We call it the hall slide.

With a running start, you hit the mattress hard and the air inside kind of shoots out the seams, propelling you forward. If you land just right, it shoots out the back and you go even faster. The initial start is crucial to the success of your distance on the hall slide. If you run far enough and fast enough and jump on the sweet spot, you can practically hover over the runway for a few seconds. The lighter guys skim right over that thing—they're flying. I'm no physicist, but it's a fun exercise in aerodynamics. Some guys are so good at it, they slide from one end of the hallway to the telephone on the wall near the other end. We're playing chicken, too—sliding at the same time from opposite ends, coming at each other with nowhere to swerve and collision imminent. I guess this seems stupid to a mature adult, but it's springtime in Saskatchewan and we're teenage boys.

I don't know who starts it, but somebody grabs a bottle of disinfectant spray that we're supposed to be using to clean the rooms, and he starts spraying people. I grab a bottle to defend myself and so does another guy, and next thing you know we have the tops off and we're splashing the full contents at one another. I go into the cleaning room and grab the short black rubber hose that we use to fill the mop bucket and turn it on, spraying water onto the floor and down the hallway. And the wet mattress pads are super slick. We're in bare feet with our shirts off and guys are practically flying across the floor, crashing into each other and screaming and laughing. The water on our bare flesh is far superior to those dry mattresses.

Dutch, a tall drink of water from the Netherlands whose family includes a few Olympians, fills up the mop bucket all the way to the top. He's getting ready to pour it out like an ocean wave down that narrow hallway. Then two of the house leaders, Shane Fort and Berry Holland show up. They're yelling at us and telling us to clean up the mess or we're going to be in a lot of trouble. But we're all hollering at Dutch to dump the water. Meanwhile, Shane and Berry are standing back, saying he better not, but we keep cheering him on, louder and louder.

"Come on, *do it*! DO IT! Dump that bucket NOW!"

Dutch gets this big grin and he lets it go. Everybody's jumping up and down like a bunch of lunatics. The water comes at us and I feel it on my toes and under my feet. That does it. The ticklish sensation activates something and the boys grab whatever they can get their hands on—cups, buckets, bottles, plastic bags, *their mouths*—and fill them with water, then they dump it on the ground.

"Stop right now! Right! Now!" Shane and Berry are pissed, but it's too late. We've gone too far and there's nothing left to do but throw caution to the wind and make it worse. Some of the wilder guys strip naked, and somebody gets the shampoo from the bathroom and squirts it all over the floor, a new level of slippery.

There's me and this redhead from Toronto, Dale Marks, who's short, strong, and carries himself like a switchblade. We create a new kind of slide that we call "the seal." This wouldn't work on the dry mattresses, but with all the water and the disinfectant and the shampoo, we can run and slide with our hands behind our backs, wiggling our bodies to push forward and barking like seals. After about a dozen of these seal runs, I'm a little tired and the fun starts to wind down for everybody.

I'm not so worried about dorm room general because everybody's involved in the ultimate hall slide, so no one's going to pass inspection. We're going to get a workout, but we're all in it together.

* * *

Monday morning comes, and it's not six, but five o'clock when we have to get up. The workout is a bad one. I don't even know how I'm going to stay awake the rest of the day. After class, I go back to the dorm and there's a sign posted that says we have a dorm meeting with Marcy. Oh jeez, this is going to be a long one. But I'm not worried. Marcy's always full of empty threats. I give her credit for creativity, but her scare tactics aren't very effective.

We file into Marshall Center and I'm pleasantly surprised to find a bunch of dressed-up eleventh- and twelfth-grade girls standing there. This is definitely not the way to make a group of ninth-grade boys feel bad. Marcy launches into her discipline speech, but I don't hear anything she's saying because all I can see are glossy lips and soft-looking hair.

This is the most trouble we've gotten in this year, but it's by far the best meeting with Marcy due to the eye candy. Then she drops the big bomb that's supposed to make us feel bad: because of our atrocious behavior, she can't accompany the girls to the rugby tournament. And since no one else can take her place, the girls can't go to the tournament at all. Maybe I should feel bad, but I'm too busy staring at Kelly Carmen, who's one of the best-looking girls in the school. She and all the other girls are supposed to be upset, but I can tell they're avoiding eye contact with us to keep from laughing. They can't be mad. It's just way too funny.

Marcy says we're the worst-behaved ninth-grade class in the history of the school, the worst fifteen-year-olds she's ever seen at Notre Dame. (Except for me, who's sixteen now because I enjoyed the fifth grade so much that I did it twice.) Marcy says we're not Hounds—we're wild dogs.

I don't feel bad and I don't think anyone else does either. We flooded Edith Hall, and they don't know who to pin the blame on because so many students were involved. But maybe we should feel bad because we didn't just flood our floor. The Marshall Center's a split-level building with offices in the basement. That means overhead lights, furniture, computers...all soaked. Yikes, it's a real mess.

Right now, we're just smirking at each other. We're all in trouble, and the seniors are in hot water too because they didn't do anything to stop it. But there's no one kid singled out for punishment.

This is probably the last big prank of my first year. It's been a big year with lots to make me laugh and cry and question everything. And even though I don't like going to school, I've learned a lot. I've made some good friends and learned about loyalty and respect and about not giving up. I lost weight too—probably from all the workouts—and I'm more confident in myself. Rodeo Day seems like a million years ago. I'm ready for the next step. I'm ready for a new dorm with more kids, more floors, and more fun. I can't wait for summer to be over so I can start my second year as an old boy.

Chapter 8

Leaner (the Fake Kid)

 hief is hands down the most hated houseparent in the whole school. If he's around, a good day immediately turns bad. His daughter is in my class, and she's nothing like him. She's intelligent, attractive, and bound to succeed. Sucks that she has such a hard-ass jerk for a dad, but oh well, like we all say, "You can't pick your parents."

You can't pick your houseparents either, and this year, in grade ten, we got Chief. You can tell when he's on duty because he runs the place like a prison. Chief's idea of an alarm clock is a piercing whistle at the crack of dawn so loud it wakes up everybody in Fred Hill.

So I'm up, and I stumble into the shower room all groggy and disoriented. Chief does the roster call like a prison guard, and the room fills up with a bunch of grade-ten and -eleven boys. We're jostling for position in line, hoping to get in before the water gets too cold. This isn't like Edith Hall, where there are fewer kids and everybody practically has their own shower. Fred Hill is packed, and the showers are like an assembly line with one guy out, another guy in, one after another. Standing in line, eyes closed, half-awake with my head resting against the ceramic tile, I know the water's already lukewarm and I'm wondering how cold it's going to be when I get in there. I'm waiting for someone to yell that it's my turn, but instead, I hear a familiar voice: it's Jubes.

"Somebody needs to teach that asshole a lesson." He's talking about Chief, obviously, the biggest drill sergeant at Notre Dame.

Jubes and me are kind of alike—a couple of pranksters and troublemakers—so we get along well. On our own, we can stir up some mischief, but get us together, and all bets are off. We're lethal.

I tilt my head away from the cold tile and open my eyes to see Jubes standing there.

"Yeah, man," I say. *I'm all in.*

I'm awake less than twenty minutes and I hear that other voice again—the one I don't want to hear.

"Hurry up. Let's rock and roll! Move!" Ugh...this guy is the worst. Somebody yells it's my turn for the shower, and sure enough, the hot water is long gone. I'm in and out of that cold water fast, then I rush to get my clothes on and head over to Assembly.

Assembly is a fancy word for all the morning announcements. It's every weekday morning in Varsity, which is the cafeteria and also the auditorium. After that, the day drags on. Not paying attention in class can get exhausting. I'm still thinking about what Jubes said in the showers about teaching Chief a lesson. After classes, I have rugby practice, and I still can't focus. My mind is working, trying to come up with a plan to get back at Chief for making dorm life hell for me and the boys.

After practice, I'm back in my room when Jubes strolls in and spends hours, *hours*, ranting about Chief. Lights out is usually around ten p.m., but you know Chief—he has to keep a tight lid on things, so for us, it's nine-thirty. I whisper to the guys that we need to talk about this more, so let's meet up in the lounge at ten. It's easy to get permission as long as you're going to study, so we each grab some binders, pencils, and maybe a textbook for cover. Our little meeting is good to go.

Now apparently, some of the guys don't know what we're up to, so they're actually studying, but it doesn't take much to get their attention. Pretty soon, we're all thinking of ways to get back at Chief. We come up with some ideas, like a barnyard door slam, for instance. Here's how it works: each guy picks their favorite farm animal. At the set time, we all holler out that animal's sound at the top of our lungs. So the cow guy moos really loud, the pig guy squeals...you get the picture. The best part about this prank is that the only person who hears the entire barnyard orchestra is the person being pranked. Everyone else is so loud, they only hear themselves. Just before the barnyard noises, we do a door slam—that's our signal. The way this works is we all disconnect the little hydraulic door closer from our doors—the thing that uses air pressure so the door doesn't slam—and then we all slam our doors at the same time. If you're in the hallway, it's enough to make your ears bleed.

This probably seems dumb, but the target wakes up to a sound louder than a gunshot followed by like fifty different animal noises. It's supposed to be farm animals, but sometimes the boys get so worked up or they just run out of animals to pick, so, you know, they just start cursing, followed by a few dolphin chirps and pheasant crows. The point is, that door slam is a lot louder than Chief's rusty high-pitched whistle, and the animal noises will terrify the hell out of anybody.

So our plan is hatched, but not quite, because Chief is a special kind of dictator who deserves more than a barnyard door slam. That's when Laser pipes up, "I know! Let's give him a leaner." Now Laser is from the Northwest Territories. He's the fastest kid on campus. But what he's saying is crazy. We all look at him with our eyes wide and tell him he's playing with a broken stick. He can't be serious, right?

In case you never heard of it, a leaner is when you fill up a garbage can with water, lean it against somebody's door, and knock. Then you beat it because as soon as that door opens, the target gets all that water dumped on them. It's simple, hilarious, never gets old, and always works. But it's not a trick you play on a houseparent. You just wouldn't.

We're all looking at each other like, "Is he serious?"

But you know me. I say, "Okay, who's going to run it?" By that, I mean who's going to knock on the door. "Me and Kisell will get it set up, but you should run it, Laser."

He just looks at me and grins. "You read my mind," he says.

The plan's getting better and better. It's late now, and Chief's probably asleep. We're really going to do this. We decide to upgrade the leaner from a knee-high trash can to a full-size one that's higher than my waist. It's rectangle-shaped, which is a good thing because when we fill it up and lean it against the door, this trash can is so heavy with water that it's bulging out at the sides. A round one would have collapsed under the weight. I'm standing in the hallway and I can see Laser. The emergency light's reflecting off his blond hair and he's got his shirt off. He's lacing up his shoes, then bouncing on his toes to get loose. The only worry at this point is how fast Chief opens that door. Laser needs time to get away.

Kisell says, "We need a distraction—something to get Chief's attention so he doesn't zero in on Laser." He's right. What if we make, like, a fake person and stick it in the hallway? That might buy Laser some time.

If we're going to go through all this trouble, we have to make sure nobody gets caught, or it's not a win. It's got to be perfect. Laser's got to get away. So as extra insurance, we all grab some random items from our rooms—a plaid shirt, a roll of white hockey tape, a football, a coat hanger, some duct tape, a Sharpie, and a broken hockey stick. We make this scarecrow-looking thing out of all this stuff, and Chester is born. He's no work of art, but we're proud of him. He's got a football for a head and he doesn't even have legs. But to us, he's perfect. We figure if we stick him down the hall a ways, with the dim lighting...he might work. Since Chester only has an upper body, we decide to put him behind a pillar, like he's peeking out. By now, it's the middle of the night and Chief must be fast asleep. Chester's in place, and we got the garbage can full of water leaning perfectly against Chief's door. Oh, and by the way, everyone in the dorm hears us tip-toeing around and they all catch on to what's going down. The guys in the upstairs dorm come down the stairwell and are prepared to hide Laser in their rooms if they have to. These guys don't like Chief either, and he isn't even their houseparent. By now, every single door is cracked open slightly, faces peeking out, eyes wide, waiting for us to make our move.

It's go time. I walk a little way down the hall to get closer to the houseparents' room. Then I give Laser the okay with my thumb and index finger, topped off with a wide-faced wink.

I slip into a dorm room and close the door to just a crack so I can watch. Laser slowly makes his way toward the houseparents' room. He's like a gladiator entering the ring. He doesn't look nervous or scared at all. All eyes are on him. I think we're about to witness something beyond my wildest imagination.

Laser's at the door. Bang, bang, bang. He knocks—hard. "Chief," he says, "I'm sick. I need Tylenol."

I feel a breeze on my face. Laser blows past me like a flash and slips around the corner at the end of the hall and out of sight. Everyone waits. With bated breath. Nothing happens. Nothing.

Chief must be a heavy sleeper. But Laser can't knock again. That would be a death wish. It's so quiet. You could hear a pin drop. Seconds turn to minutes and I'm fully prepared to shut this thing down. From the looks of it, so is everyone else.

Laser comes out of hiding and I'm about to open my mouth and commend him on his attempt. *Oh well*, I'm thinking, *we tried.*

But Laser hisses, pounding a fist into his open hand, "I didn't do all this work to go to bed empty-handed. We're getting this bastard if it's the last thing we do."

Wow. I am not about to get in the way of a man on a mission. I stand back. Laser walks up to the door (which seems to take forever, but that must just be the suspense) and bangs a lot louder than the first time.

"Chief!" he hollers. "I'm really sick. I need Tylenol!" He's off again and I feel that old familiar breeze on my face.

Chief finally comes to the door. He opens it, the leaner drops like a tsunami, and he gets pummeled with water. Get this: he's standing there wearing nothing but a pair of moccasins and tighty-whities that are three sizes too small. He looks ridiculous. And really pissed. I have a clear view and can see him shaking his head. Then he starts yelling.

"Well," he says, like he's totally disgusted, "isn't that just wonderful!" He's so loud that everyone can hear him. I can't believe I'm looking at this middle-aged man in this outfit, soaking wet with his face all red and screwed up like he's going to blow a gasket. I'm laughing so hard that no sound is coming out. This is priceless. It's the best.

Then Chief spots Chester the "fake kid" peeking out from behind the pillar. He starts yelling at him.

"Wipe that smile off your face," he bellows. Chester's still smiling. "Are you deaf? Or just plain stupid?" Another pause. "God help you if I come down there," he hollers.

Chester is still grinning from ear to ear, holding his ground. Now I've seen a lot. I saw the Colosseum in Rome. I saw the Rolling Stones in concert. Those things pale in comparison to what's going on in front of my eyes. Chief barrels down the hallway like an angry lion hunting his prey. By the time he figures out what's going on, he's furious. I can feel the heat of his anger all the way to the end of the hallway. Then he just puts his hands on his hips and shakes his head like he's baffled and downright embarrassed. Chester, meanwhile, is still grinning, but Chief is not in the mood. He grabs the coat hanger and throws it on the ground. Then he drags poor old Chester's lifeless body down the hall and back to his room. We had hope, saw courage and potential in Chester's future. And just like that, Chief crushed his dreams...and ours.

Before Chief can say another word, every door slams. It's loud. Because the leaner and the fake kid aren't enough. It's a good old barnyard door slam. Everybody makes their barnyard animal noises, full volume, and we're all laughing, tears streaming down our faces. Right now, in this moment, nothing else matters. Not divorced parents or failing grades. Everyone is living in this moment together, and we are pissing ourselves laughing.

After a while, we all make our way to bed. Everyone's amazed by how well the plan unfolded. That night's going down as one of the best pranks during my time in the dorm. Laser's a hero. It was legendary: Laser – 1, Chief – 0.

Six o'clock rolls around too soon and Chief's already screaming.

"Get up! Get your asses up and out of bed right now!" Most of us knew this was coming, but this one group of guys was out of town for a hockey game and they don't know what's happening. These poor bastards played a three-period game, came back to campus in the middle of the night on a bus, and they're in trouble. They're guilty by association, and they don't even know why.

We're all in the hallway and Chief's there with backup. It's houseparent John Woodsmere, and he's demanding answers. They're just looking for someone to pin this on, someone to blame, shame, and punish. They want to make an example out of somebody. They want to teach us a lesson. The group's airtight. We're a family, and no one's breathing a word. We don't snitch. Ever.

Chief gets in my face, and John is right behind him. They're bellowing.

"Tell me who did it! Tell me who it was right now, you little shit!" Past the two of them, I can see that Chief's door is wide open. Chester's lying there in a mangled heap on Chief's bed. I can see the plaid shirt and the hockey tape hanging in shreds and I burst out laughing. I can't help it. I can't even breathe, I'm laughing so hard. Chief keeps yelling and John looks furious, but I can't stop. It's hilarious.

Chief backs off me and his eyes go big. He looks up and down the hall at all the guys.

"Okay, boys, since nobody wants to admit it, you're all going to be punished. Everyone get over to the gym. I'll be there shortly. NOW MOVE. GO!"

We all head out the door and run across campus to the gymnasium, giggling the whole way. We want to get there before Chief. We want to all make sure no one's going to tell.

We hustle inside, and Laser says, "I'll take it, boys. I'll take the blame." But everyone's got the same look on their face. No one's going to let Laser take the fall. Not a chance. We're in this together.

Everyone's nodding and saying, "Hell no, buddy, not a chance." This is coming from a platoon of about thirty-five strong. I hear Chief and John coming. They're talking about a workout as they come in through the door. *What are they going to do to us this time?*

What follows is the hardest workout I've ever done at Notre Dame. Ever. We all sit on the bench and Chief does a head count. He tells us to get on the line, which is the taped line across the floor along the wall. There's taped lines on two sides, and Chief tells us we're doing "suicides," running back and forth from one side of the gym to the other. We get to about twenty laps and you can tell guys are getting worn out. These aren't easy laps we have to run, and after last night's shenanigans, I'm pretty tired.

Then Laser yells out, "Okay, it was me!"

One guy, then another, yells "No, it was me!"

Now everyone's yelling, "It was me! It was me!" There's sweat streaming down our faces and we're tired, but nobody wants Laser to take the fall.

"Oh, so you boys like playing games." Chief's taunting us. Being his usual self. "Okay," he says. "Let's play some games."

Chief doesn't get it. This isn't about games. It's about loyalty. We're all guilty as hell; we all had a hand in the stunt. Laser just made it possible. No one's going to let him take the blame.

Now we're forty laps deep into this shit, shirts off, and the place reeks of sweat. But there's no chance Chief's letting up. We have to get to fifty laps no matter what. He's treating us like sled dogs.

"The longer it takes you rats to finish your laps, the longer you're going to be here," he says.

There's ten of us left, and I can't even talk. One guy keels over. His legs just collapse and he's done.

Laser yells out again, "I did it! It was me!" He adds more, "And I'm glad I did it!"

The other guys chime in again, "It was me, it was me!" I try to yell too but my mouth is so dry, all I can do is wave my hand and moan.

Chief tells everyone to get off the court. Everyone but Laser. Chief wants him to keep running. The rest of us drop to the floor like soldiers on a battlefield, wiped out, soaking wet, and defeated. I'm breathing in and out, deep slow breaths, trying to get my heart rate down and not vomit like others already have.

Laser's running even harder now, and he's running his mouth too. "You're not going to break me! I can do this all day," he says.

Man, is Chief pissed. He tells Laser to sprint faster, and Laser just smiles and obliges. By now, most of us have regained our composure and we're just watching Laser in awe. His determination is inspiring. I can see John talking to Chief. He's pointing at his watch, probably telling him that we need to wrap this up so we can all get showered and dressed and get to Assembly by eight. This battle is over, but something tells me the war will rage on.

I can't wait for lunch hour to take a nap. I find out later that Laser's been rewarded with a three-day in-school suspension. Nobody ever tells, and Chief still doesn't know who was behind it all. But he had to blame somebody.

I run over to Laser during class change. "Hey man," I say. "Tough break."

"Are you kidding me?" he laughs, "I'd do it all over again."

During my next class, I look out the window and stare at Laser shoveling the snow off the pathway. That's what they do to you for in-school suspension—make you work with the grounds crew. He's still smiling. 2–0 final, Laser wins.

Chapter 9

Food Fight

arsity's one of my favorite places on campus because that's where we eat. I love to eat. Period.

The rules for the lunch line are simple. Grades eleven and twelve roll through first, collecting their nourishment for the afternoon. After about twenty or thirty minutes, the grade-nine and -ten kids can line up to fill their plates and trays. The system eases traffic, and even though I'm in grade ten, I'm cool with most of the older students, so they don't make a big deal when I get in line early.

When you walk into Varsity, there are four rows of tables on each side of the room, half on the left and half on the right, with an aisle down the middle. There's red carpet on either side with dollies for trays, cups, plates, and silverware that you grab before getting in line. You get your utensils and go to the left or the right. Then you wait for your turn at the serving station. Sometimes you talk to the other guys in line, or just look around, and sometimes you stare at Jesus.

Hanging on the cafeteria wall is this huge painting of our Lord and Savior. He's on the cross, looking down on all of us. That painting's got to be at least ten feet tall and six feet wide. It's massive. He watches over us at every meal.

One of the tables on the right side of the room—the one closest to the lunch line—is a staff table. There's a different staff member on duty every day, and their job is simple: make sure no one causes any shit during lunchtime. Today it's Vince, but he's nowhere to be seen. Other than the Chosen One and the kitchen staff in the back that are bringing out more food, no one's got their eye on us. It's just students.

As usual, everyone's sitting with their groups. Even though this is a small school with only about 300 students, it has a lot of cliques, and people tend to hang with their respective groups and not mix. It's not like they have any problems with each other—they just keep to themselves around campus and in Varsity. The midget triple-A team sits together and the non-hockey kids like Sticks and Leewig sit together. Younger kids don't sit with upperclassmen. Guys don't typically eat with girls.

Today all the older students are on the left side of the room, in line or sitting down to eat. I'm on the right side with the younger guys. The girls are on this side too. There's maybe thirty people on this side. And for once, I'm minding own business. I have my head down and I'm focused on one thing: lunch. It's Fish Friday, so I'm loaded up with fish sticks, French fries, and cole slaw.

I catch something out of the corner of my eye. It flies by in the air overhead. A few seconds later, something else flies by. I look over at the older student's side and see Lex Stenson, a grade-eleven kid. Lex is tall and tough, from Saskatchewan—a fighter first, a hockey player second. He's really fit and can handle himself with the best of them. He's laughing pretty hard, and looking over at another table where Sticks, Leewig, and Trunk are sitting.

Sticks yells, "Oh yeah?" and grabs a bunch of food off his plate and throws it straight at Lex. Not just one fish stick but, like, a whole handful of sloppy wet food. Straight at Lex.

And just like that, food is everywhere. Not just fish sticks and fries, either, which are surprisingly aerodynamic, but chocolate milk, cole slaw, lettuce, mustard, beets, carrots, olives, ranch dressing, bread buns, tartar sauce, honey, salt and pepper shakers, and cottage cheese. Grilled cheese sandwiches, tomato soup, and salad. There is food everywhere. It looks like a rainbow. I can't even see across the room. I can't see the walls. Then plates start flying, and forks, knives, and spoons. I am honestly frightened. This is petrifying. It seemed to happen in slow motion, from my brain, a fish stick and fry meeting in the middle, almost like they're elegantly ballroom dancing with one another.

In all the flying food, I make brief eye contact with Lex and his eyes go wide, like he's going for a big hit on the ice. He picks up his tray, with all the food and utensils on board, and flips it straight over his head so hard it flies across the room and smashes onto a table a couple of rows down. By now, some of the guys have smartened up. They don't want to get blamed for this mess, and they're running for the door. Some people at the far end dip low and escape through the back door of the kitchen. Brilliant departure.

This might be a good time to make my exit, but here's the principal, Owen Peters, coming through the front door. Now Owen's a former college football athlete, and even though he's in his forties, he could still compete with kids half his age on the gridiron. He's so big, the wave of hockey players charging past him for the door doesn't even phase him, and he grabs one of them by the arm: *Sticks*. Now to be honest, everyone on that side of the room is responsible for what's going down. But it's kind of ironic that the one guy Owen grabs, Sticks, is the one who started it, or at least took it to this level. Sticks has whipped cream on his face and a long line of red. I can't tell if it's ketchup or blood, but he's screaming that he got hit in the head with a plate.

Owen's still got him by the arm and he's bellowing, "Who threw the plate?" He looks around and you can tell that he's just now seeing the mess. It looks like a food bomb exploded, especially on the left side of the room. And all the kids have cleared out from that side except one, Torch, this short guy with bright orange hair from Calgary, Alberta. I can't figure out for the life of me why he didn't run when he had the chance. Torchy's got this huge grin plastered on his face, but he's not looking toward the door and he doesn't see Owen. In his supreme ignorance of the situation, he whips a cup of chocolate milk across the room. And he's laughing, even though all the other kids are gone and the chocolate milk just bounces off a table and hits the floor. So not only did he waste the throw, he just got caught red-handed after the worst food fight in Notre Dame history.

Owen barks at Torch, "What the hell happened here?" but he doesn't wait for an answer. "Never mind—kitchen! Get a hairnet on and start cleaning this shit up." Torch hops to it, and Owen storms out, probably to go after some of the other guys. Because it's obvious us younger guys and the girls didn't do this and Torch didn't do it all by himself. Helen comes in and she's one of the best teachers at ND. She's tending to Stick's face, and she says he's going to need stitches.

I feel like I just witnessed a historic day at Notre Dame. All because Vince, the houseparent, was late for lunch duty. He left us alone with no adult supervision, no one watching over us.

Except Him. Because Jesus is still up there on the wall staring down at the mess. The silent witness. There's a smear of mustard under one of his armpits. It's yellow now, but I bet it dries brown, like a sweat stain. No one's going to clean that off; it's too high. That stain will be there forever.

Unless you were there, you'd never believe this food fight. Unless you saw all that food all over the floor, the walls, the chairs, the windows, you would never believe anyone could get that much food in the air. But that mustard stain under Jesus's armpit is all the proof I need of the greatest food fight that ever was.

Chapter 10

A Rock and a Hard Place

I trust Abs never to rat on me. After all, he roomed with me all through the ninth grade. I had my dorm room switched a few times that year due to getting in trouble, but Abs was always switched right along with me. We were always in hot water too, but we had each other's backs, and it's no different in grade ten. Abs is in B-1 and I'm in B-3, the two rooms closest to the houseparents' room. That's no surprise, given our history. To be honest, I don't really mind. Torchy's in B-1 with Abs. They're friends from back home in Calgary, where they're from.

After a few weeks off campus for Easter vacation, it's back to school. We're in the dorm tonight and supposed to be winding down for lights out, but Abs and Torchy are fiddling around with something in Abs's locker. I'm trying to see what they're up to, but they're blocking my view, clearly hiding something from me.

"Let's show him," says Torchy, but Abs says, "No, no." They go back and forth like that until I'm pleading like a toddler. I want to see what they have. Finally, Abs gives in and stretches out his hand, then slowly opens it. In his palm, there are these tiny pills—a yellow one, a blue one, and some white ones. The blue one is triangle-shaped. Before I can touch them, he closes his fist and pulls it away.

"I took them from my dad's office," Abs says with a smirk. His dad's a doctor.

"What do they do?" I demand. "I need answers!"

"They're for a good night's rest," he says.

"Well, then I want one!" I say. Of course, I want one. Why should I be denied the luxury of prime sleep? I put my hand out. "Give it to me."

Abs says, "No, they're for me."

"Please, just one," I'm begging him.

Abs says, "I swear, if you tell anyone..."

"Give me a break, man! You know I won't." Like I said, we never rat.

Abs starts to cave. "How heavy do you want to sleep?" he says.

I tell him, "The heaviest," and he says, "Okay, take this one," and hands me the blue pill. I take a swig of Gatorade and down the pill. Abs has a devilish look on his face like he knows something I don't.

"Hey Christos," says Torchy, as he lays sprawled out on his bed, hands clasped behind his head. "You just took Viagra." He lets out this high-pitched squeal. He's laughing like it's a big joke, which doesn't surprise me because Torchy loves a good prank. But it's not a big deal and I just shrug it off. I'm not even mad because these are my friends and Viagra is for old men. I'm a young healthy teenager. I don't need any assistance in that department. It won't even affect me.

So I'm back in my room, in bed, having the usual chit-chat with the guys. There's Marty and Tim, who I've known since freshman year. A couple of older guys from upstairs are there too—Grozzy, who's in his eleventh year, is rough around the edges and demands our respect.

Things quiet down after a while, and I can tell everyone's dosing off, but I can't get comfortable. I'm tossing and turning, and

I get up and pace around the room, lie down again, sit up on the bed and tap my feet, clap my hands. I'm breathing heavily. Something's not right. The lights have been out for a good thirty minutes now, and it's getting worse. I have the sweats and I'm light-headed. There's no way I'm sleeping. I walk over to Abs and Torchy's room and tell them I can't sleep. My voice is choppy and I'm breathing harder now. Torch jumps up and turns on the light.

"Is it working?" he says, then. "Whoa!" He's slapping his hand on the pillow and pointing at me. I look down at my shorts and it all makes sense—the knot in my stomach, the shakiness. Abs is awake but he's not laughing. I'm all sweaty and panting, not to mention the obvious. He has an uneasy look on his face.

"Make it go away!" he hollers at me. I'm too out of it to even respond, but I'm thinking, *Sure, pal, like I'm doing this on purpose.* I wish I could take a time machine back to an hour ago and never step foot in their room. Never take that little blue pill. It doesn't take Torchy long to get a lot of other guys from around the dorm to come marvel at my predicament and, of course, laugh at my expense. They're all asking me questions, but I need air. I'm overheating, panicking now. I try to leave the room, but I can see John Woodsmere coming down the hallway. John is round, stocky, and irritable, and he doesn't like being bothered when he's not on regular houseparent duty—or when he is, for that matter. He looks right at me and I quickly drop down and turn to hide my midsection.

John gets down into my face. "What the hell's going on?" he says.

"I'm sick," I tell him, but John's smart enough to know that with this crowd of hyenas around me, heckling and laughing, there's something else going on.

"Kalogirou," he says lightly, "you don't look sick, and all your pals seem to think that whatever's going on is pretty humorous, so why don't you just speed up the process of your stupidity and tell me what's up so we can all get back to sleep."

John's good at getting me to come clean. Nobody else on campus—and I mean nobody—can get inside my head like he can. Besides, right now I need his help. I don't know what to do. I don't know if I need medical attention and I don't know if I'll get in trouble. I don't know if this will all blow over or if it's going to last forever. John puts his left hand on my sweat-soaked back and takes a knee.

"Just tell me," he says. And now I'm stuck between a rock and a hard place. Literally.

"I took Viagra," I tell him, and flop over onto my back. Now I'm dizzy, probably from the panic. Some guys are howling, but others are stunned.

"Oh, for Christ's sake. You've got to be kidding me. Where did you get it?"

Before I can answer, Abs steps up and says, "I gave it to him. I didn't think it would do anything. I screwed up."

John doesn't seem concerned, but I can tell he's embarrassed because now he has to call the ladies at the health center and explain the problem. And that the usual suspects are to blame—again. I tell him he doesn't have to call them, that I'll be fine, but he says he has to as a precaution. He takes what seems like forever to spit the words out over the phone. I can hear him out in the hallway as I'm lying on the carpet in a terrible state.

Then he finally says to us, "Okay, morons, this is going to last a few hours. So lights out; the party's over."

Everyone snickers as they leave to walk back to their rooms and I go back to mine. I can hear their voices moving away down the hall as I sit beside the door with my overheated back against the cold, white wall. Abs follows me, probably because he feels pretty bad about what he just put me through. I'm embarrassed, sure, but I'm so glad to hear that I'm going to be all right.

"G'night, bro," I say to Abs as he heads back to his room.

"Yeah, good night," he says. "Try not to stay up too late." I'm in B-3 now, curled up on my bed like an overcooked shrimp.

John's standing in the doorway, and he shakes his head and smirks. Then he says, "You're something else. I'll get you some water." My roommates are concerned about me but are smiling too, and rightfully so. I don't blame them. I'm sure I would be laughing too.

John knows how dumb I feel, and we both know how fast word will get around campus the next day. I'll be the center of attention until something else happens to take the focus off myself. Anyway, nothing to do now but wait.

* * *

The next day is a long one with jokes directed at me from students and staff members. Everyone's got to get their jabs in, it seems. It's nice to get back to my room, but I'm worried about the punishment that awaits me and Abs. Whatever it is, it can't be as bad as a teacher saying, "Kalogirou, what were you up to last night?"

John dishes out hours for what's being billed as different forms of disrespect. "Abs," he says, "you're getting thirty-two hours for drug abuse. Christos, you're getting sixteen hours for a new category we're going to call 'gullibility'." I'm probably better off than Abs because now he has to call his dad and tell him he took prescription pills from his office. That guy is strict—the kind of dad who demands excellence from his son both on the ice and

Athol Murray
College of
Notre Dame

1. Fred Hill, Max Bell Dorms
2. Seaman Hall
3. Mother Teresa Hall
4. Tower of God
5. St. Agustine's Church
6. Edith Hall
7. Duncan McNeil Arena
   and Gymnasium
8. Museum / Archives
9. Varsity Dining Hall
10. McCusker Hall
11. Mayard House
12. White House
13. Carr Hall
14. Maintenance Center
15. Hound Shop
16. Lane Hall
17. Art Room
18. President's House
19. The White Church
20. Smoke Pit
21. The Dugout
22. Baseball Diamond
23. Football Field
24. Healthcare Center
25. Town Rink

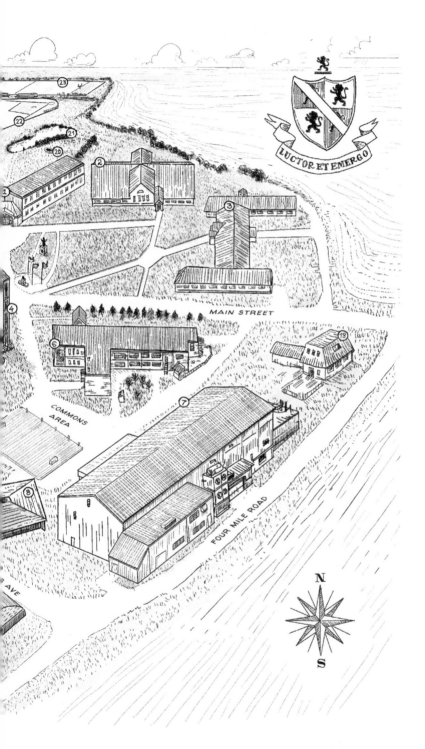

LUCTOR ET EMERGO

MAIN STREET

COMMONS AREA

FOUR MILE ROAD

AVE

N

S

in the classroom. By comparison, I'm getting off easy, even with jokes being thrown my way for the next little while.

This isn't the first time I learned the hard way, and I have a feeling it won't be the last. But it's the first time I've been literally stuck between a rock and a hard place.

Chapter 11

Dirty Bob and the Infamous Dog Pound

t's after midnight on a weekend, and everyone's settled into rooms to sleep or watch movies with their roommates or dorm mates from other rooms. I'm walking back to my room from the bathroom, just minding my own business, when I smell something. It's a strong, distinctive smell, and I'm trying to place what it is and where it's coming from. I stop at the door of the houseparents' office and figure they're probably asleep, but I can't know for sure. I press my ear to the metal door and I can hear them snoring away. Out like a light. The smell's not coming from there, and even though I'm just a few meters from my room, I have to know.

Hands on my hips, I do the same sniff test with B-1. Nothing. I'm baffled. I walk over to the emergency exit to the outer hallway, press my nose into the gap between the big double doors, and breathe deep, as my nose goes up and down the slit. That's the smell. *Where's it coming from?* I know if I go out those doors an alarm will go off and wake up the houseparents, so I pass for now. I get in enough trouble and I don't need any more.

I walk around some more but keep coming back to these doors. I'm restless and I have to know what that stench is—it's killing me. I get some money from my room as insurance so if someone in authority catches me in the hallway after lights out, I can just say I was thirsty and heading over to the pop machine for a drink. I pull open one of the double doors and wait a minute or so. It makes a buzzing noise, but there's no alarm, and after another minute, it stops. Nobody's coming, so I guess nobody woke up.

The smell's stronger as I head for the lobby and check the soda machine to see if it's burning plastic from the surge protector. Nope. I walk over to the glass doors that open to the shortcut to the football field and baseball diamonds. The walls here are floor-to-ceiling plates of glass, and I put my face to the glass to see into the dark on the other side. There's nothing out there. Then I head over to the grade-twelve boot room to check out their pop machine, and I catch a strong whiff of the smell. It's coming from the grade-twelve dorm. I shouldn't be up roaming

92

around in the middle of the night, and I definitely shouldn't be in the link[9]—which is the common area that connects the two dorm wings—after lights out, let alone the grade-twelve dorms. I throw caution to the wind and keep going. Here goes nothing.

I creep right up to the door that leads to the dorms and take a huge whiff from the bottom of the doors to the top. Finally, it clicks. I know that smell—it's cigar smoke! I recognize it from spending time with my Italian uncles in Montreal. The last time I stayed with them for the summer, I actually started reading *Cigar Aficionado* magazine. I know more about cigars than I probably should for a teenager, and the smell is definitely distinguishable from cigarette smoke.

Now it's not like smoking isn't allowed at all, but you have to be old enough and you have to have a smoking card or parental permission. Then you can smoke in the picnic area outside between Max Bell and Fred Hill. I go over to the doors that lead outside and put my hands to the glass like binoculars and press my eyes into them. I have a clear view of the picnic table area in front of Fred Hill. Nope, nobody. So whoever's smoking has to be inside and they have to be crazy because the odds of not getting caught are slim to none. I mean, I could smell the smoke all the way over in my dorm in the opposite wing.

I open the doors and there's a beep-beep-beep—the alarm going off—but I don't care if I get caught. I have to see what's going on.

The first door I come to is the houseparents', and I'm trying to be quiet, but the door opens and there's Dirty Bob.

Bob isn't your typical houseparent. He's a hippie, and I can't confirm this, but it's rumored he smokes weed with the guys. I find this very badass and humorous. He also says the word "bitchin'" a lot, which I think is very cool. Bob has big sloppy hair and he's got bad body odor like a skunk, and I never could understand how this guy got hired to be a houseparent in the first place.

"If you're looking for the party," he whispers in a raspy voice, "it's down the hall. Last door on your right." He points a long skinny finger in that direction. Bob's a cool guy, but he's supposed to be in charge, and letting the guys have a party—and worse, telling me, a tenth-grader, where it is—is beyond anything I can imagine. The further I walk down the hall, the stronger the smell. I can hear and feel the vibrating bass of music as I get closer and closer. It's dark, and I press my hand against the cinder block wall, sliding it across till I come to the door. There's a torn piece of paper taped to the door, bouncing to the music. Written in sloppy crayon-spelled letters are words I will never forget: *Welcome to the Dawgpound Party*. My jaw drops like a cartoon character, not just because of the party and the cigar smoke, but because this is the Dawgpound. The infamous Dawgpound.

The Dawgpound is a group of grade-twelve guys that are the epitome of power, respect, and authority on campus. The group was formed in grade nine, and these guys have been rocking it full throttle all four years. It's easily the wildest bunch I ever encountered at school. If they give you a dirty look, you look the other way. If they call you over, you run to them. That's just how it works.

I still have my hands on the steel door, and the vibration from the bass travels through my body and reminds me of the beatdowns I got from these guys in grade nine. There's one I'll for sure never forget. I was outside Kenny Hall one time when a few of them caught me alone. The way they looked at me was like they'd just been handed an unexpected gift, the equivalent of receiving flowers from a lost love. One of the guys, an original founder of the 'Pound, looked at me with this dangerous kind of smile and signaled the group. They broke up like a pack of wolves, or more like a team of assassins. See, they wouldn't run toward you because that wouldn't be fun. By splitting up like this, they let you know there was nowhere to hide. I just wanted to surrender and take my lumps, but no, not the 'Pound. They liked the game. They wanted to hunt their prey and make the sweet smell of fear in the air burn slow. And once they closed in, fighting back wasn't even an option. You just had to give in and take your punishment. *Yes please, may I have another titty-twister? I hope it's thrilling like the last one.* I remember that beatdown, and so many others.

Since I'm older now, a grade-ten boy, they don't mess with me. I guess I paid my dues with interest last year. But am I actually on the guest list for the Dawgpound party? I know I'm cool with the 'Pound, but am I cool enough to hang? I don't know, but I want to find out. I have to open that door. A gentle push allows thick smoke to eagerly escape into the hallway.

Everything's happening in slow motion now. This isn't a four-man room in the grade-twelve dorms. It's a night out on the town with everyone wearing their best suits. It's bottle service at the Boom Boom Room. No, it's more like a concert, drawing more fans than the Wu-Tang Clan. But really, it's not any of those things. What's happening in that room is far more majestic. I push the door open wide and see that Ace is there, the only American in the crew. He's a smooth talker. Kamer's there too, from Korea, and Robby Banner, who's messed with me the least but still knows how to instigate trouble. Braden's there, the only guy on campus who's not afraid to say anything, and I mean *ANYTHING*, even to a teacher. Then there's Jackie, the golden boy in rugby. Finally, there's Dale Talltree, the eighth wonder of the world who could probably kill anybody with his bare hands. He's a teenager the size of a grain elevator. All six and a half feet and 240 pounds of him in tight boxers and sunglasses is bouncing to the beat on top of a desk that runs the length of the room under the two windows.

Layers of smoke mixed with the crisp melody of DMX's *Ruff Ryders' Anthem* filling the air. A big hand presses a cold Budweiser heavy into my palm.

"Suck it down—there aren't many left." I look at the floor, and though it's fuzzy through all the smoke plus I'm still in a daze, I see three empty thirty-packs of Budweiser. Beer cans are scattered all over like shrapnel on a battlefield. For a bunch of high schoolers at a boarding school in a small town that doesn't have anywhere to buy beer, that's impressive—no, that's especially impressive. I'm amazed by how much they've already drunk, and I'm guessing Dale is putting up the high numbers.

This is the mountain top, the pot of gold at the end of the rainbow. Here I am after all the beatings, doing my best to avoid these guys my entire first year, and now I'm not just drinking with the group, I'm partying with them. I breathe in the strong cigar smoke and know I'm not an outsider anymore. I'm one of them—an official or maybe an unofficial member of the Dawgpound. Maybe for just a short time, but still, this is glorious.

Perry, who's one of the unofficial leaders of the Dawgpound, isn't there, which makes sense to me because he's a house leader and he's probably avoiding the party so he doesn't get stripped of his house leader title. He's probably a lookout to make sure they don't get caught. I don't know this for sure, and I have no intention of asking. Truthfully, I don't even know why I'm sticking around. *Do they know who I am?*

These guys are so cool, and if this is any indication of what my senior year will look like, I can't wait. I find myself throwing out high-fives and pounds—fist bumps—at the boys before making my way out the door. I'm not overstaying my welcome.

I head back down the hallway, and before I walk through the double doors, Dirty Bob comes out and looks at me with lazy, half-opened eyes.

"Hey, Christos, did you have a good time?"

"I sure did," I reply with a grin.

* * *

The next morning isn't so pleasant. I wake up, and I can still smell the cigar smoke, but it's not in the air, it's just my clothes. I head out to find out what happened with the party and it's bad news. Dirty Bob got fired.

What he did was by far the coolest move in the history of houseparents, but I'm sure allowing and encouraging parties is frowned upon by the school. I wonder if he knew he was getting canned. Maybe that's why he told me about the party. He knew he was on his way out and just didn't care. I probably should have thanked him, but I wasn't thinking about it last night. I wasn't thinking about anything except how cool it was, for just one night, to party with the Dawgpound.

Chapter 12

The Definition of a Wingman

rom all that I've read and seen in movies, it seems like there comes a time in every young man's life when he realizes he cares for someone more than he ever thought possible. Today is that moment in my life, and that someone is Sophie Zale. I've caught Sophie staring at me during class and at hockey games, and whenever I walk by her, I can see her turn her head out of the corner of my eye. I sure like the attention. After all, I'm sixteen and she's beautiful. Cooties are a thing of the past, and girls are this whole new factor in life that make me nervous. I can't hide it around Sophie.

Sophie has a sister, Liv, who's two years above us in grade twelve. Liv's always nice to me and that makes me feel cool when she sees me. Sometimes in Varsity, she says, "Hey, Christos," when I walk past, and that puts a glow on my face. An older, pretty girl knows who I am, and that makes me look cool in front of all the other guys. Since Liv likes me, at least as a friend, I think I might have a chance with her younger sister, Sophie. Both girls play hockey, of course, because this is Notre Dame, Canada's unofficial hockey player factory. They come from a great family with good parents connected to the hockey world, to put it lightly—their father was a Hound and a legend in the sport, having represented Canada in the Olympics. Needless to say, I probably don't fit the ideal description of who this guy wants near his girls. Of course, I don't care, because I like Sophie and I can tell she likes me. Nothing else seems to matter.

Sophie's dad helps out with Notre Dame's hockey program, so they have a house in town too. They're originally from Alberta and just an all-around great family. The problem is, unlike them, I'm not big on sports. I'm also always in trouble and my grades are low, as in similar in depth to where the Titanic now rests. I'm the full package, right? Brilliant.

Sophie and I start spending a lot of time together at the end of January, but I tell her I want to keep it quiet because it's more fun if nobody knows. The truth is, Sophie's an honor student and excels at sports, while depending on who you talk to, I'm either the biggest rebel or the laughingstock of Notre Dame. I want to keep us a secret for her sake. I don't want her to catch flak from the other students or from her dad. I may not be giving my all at school, but I treat Sophie really well. Over time, she's become my best friend.

After a while, I tell a few friends here and there about Sophie and myself. But mostly, nobody knows and now it's been a few months. I don't want her to lose interest in me or think I don't care, but it's hard to show her how I feel because it's always in disguise. I need to do something spectacular to leave her completely breathless. The problem is, we're in the middle of nowhere. Wilcox has nothing but a park and two hockey rinks, so I have to get creative to wow her. What can I say, it's not like there's a wine list at Varsity.

There's this guy Hunter who I'm tight with, and I spend a lot of nights crashing on the floor in his room. We never get sick of each other, and he's full of charm. He always gives me tips on dating and is there to coach me through my relationship with Sophie. Not only that, but he's also a great hockey player and can even sing in perfect harmony to Craig David's *Born to Do It* album. I mean, this guy knows every single word to that album. Impressive.

Hunter knows I'm trying hard with Sophie, and tonight I have to see what he's thinking, so I head over to his room. Before I can even sit down, he tells me how he's figured the whole thing out. He has a full execution planned, and from the way he pitches it, I feel like I'm about to help him rob a bank.

"Here's the plan," he says, "Take Sophie out to the football field this weekend. When it gets dark, say around eight or nine o'clock, sit on the bleachers one row below the very top. I'll stand far out enough for you guys to hear me, but not so close that you can see me." He has all the details worked out and goes on to explain how it'll play out. We bounce more ideas off one another and get excited about this genius plan.

I'm waiting impatiently for Saturday to roll around, and I take a trip to the Hound Shop, which is the canteen on Main Street that sells stuff you can't get in vending machines, to get champagne flutes, which are part of the plan. Frankly, I can't believe they even sell champagne flutes at the Hound Shop.

***

It's Saturday morning, and from the moment the sun comes up, I'm thinking about the plan. I'm nervous, really nervous, and I tell Sophie that I'm going to have a surprise for her once it gets dark. I keep looking at the sun all day just wishing it would hurry up and go down already. I see Sophie again in the late afternoon, and she wants to know what this big surprise is all about anyway.

I have to admit, it feels pretty good to see her so excited. She's eager for details, but I'm not giving anything up. Finally, it's getting dark and we start our walk onto the football field. It's a little chilly, even with sweaters on in mid-May. So I get another idea and tell Sophie to wait in the baseball diamond dugout.

"I'll be right back, I promise," I tell her. Mother Nature's providing a symphony of crickets and a nice breeze that's blowing softly through the farmland around the field. Given the fact that we're out here in the middle of nowhere, the setting feels sort of like a cheesy horror movie. But in Wilcox, this is as romantic as it will ever get for a couple of tenth graders.

I run as fast as I can back to Fred Hill dorm. Just ten minutes until showtime. I don't go in through the back entrance of the building because I know it'll be crowded, and I don't want an audience. I bang on some windows, hoping someone is in their room who can grab my blanket for me. And find the worst possible candidate. Mitch Brassand is a nice kid, but he's one of the biggest guys on campus and a bit slow in more ways than one, if you know what I mean. He's definitely not my first pick to run something out to me in a timely manner. But I'm in a crunch, completely out of breath and gasping for air by the time I get to the window, so I tell him to go to B-3 and grab my cheetah print blanket without telling anyone what he's doing. He agrees to go, and I tell him—actually, I *beg* him—to move as quickly as possible.

I wait for what seems like a lifetime and watch Mitch through the windows. Now he's coming with the blanket—I can see it in his hand. The blinds to the lounge are open and I can see him stop at the pop machine. *Are you kidding me?* I'm thinking. I'm raging inside. Here I am, out of breath from running while Sophie is sitting by herself, freezing cold, out by the dugout, surrounded by millions of crickets. Meanwhile, this guy is taking his sweet-ass time. Okay, he's on the move again. Here he is now, and he struggles to shove my blanket through the tiny opening at the top of his dorm window. I don't waste any time. I grab the blanket and I'm running back to Sophie. As I run past the back end of the link, I see Hunter being heckled by a large group of guys. He's shaking it off, as usual, and focused on the job ahead. *That's Hunter,* I think. *Putting his best buddy ahead of his own problems.*

I head out to the field and get Sophie, take her hand, and walk her up to the second-to-last row of bleachers. We're both pretty much beaming with anticipation. She doesn't know what's coming, and I don't know how she'll respond. I wrap the blanket around us and we're sitting there under the stars. The moon's shining brightly above and I can still hear the crickets— that, and Sophie's breath. It's so quiet up here. I hear steps approaching.

"What's that?" Sophie says, and I laugh nervously. Now I can see him coming toward the bleachers. He's dressed in a suit, all nicely pressed like he's going to a wedding. Hunter stops at the bottom of the bleachers and looks up at us. He's got this puzzled look on his face as he climbs the steps.

"Christos? Sophie? What are you guys doing out here?" he says, playing dumb. Then he hands us a couple of Notre Dame champagne flutes, pulls out a bottle of ginger ale, and fills our glasses halfway up, like we're sitting at a fancy restaurant and he's the maître d'. He slips a pack of gum into my hand and gives me a wink as if to say, "Lights, camera, action."

I can't believe this is happening. Now Hunter gets into position and I'm thinking that I'll never forget this. It's one of those times that just sticks in your mind because it's so good.

Hunter starts singing. He's in perfect tune, of course, and he sings parts of different songs, the best parts. It's like Sophie and I are having our own private concert. We clap and laugh and cheer him on, living in the moment. It's nothing extravagant, but it's creative and from the heart.

Life at school can get so complicated. It's nice to have this time, just me and Sophie and Hunter singing his heart out, soaking up this moment. The simplicity.

The church bells from the school's nondenominational church, the Tower of God[10], seem more special tonight. They're chiming, signaling me back to the dorm. I walk Sophie to the edge of the field where it meets the road into town, the road she lives on. Sophie thanks me for such a special night, and I just stand there, not wanting it to end. I'm going to be late getting back to the dorm, but I don't care. I'd do it all over again.

I head over to my dorm with the biggest smile on my face ever. I couldn't stop smiling if I had to. The wind picks up, and it's blowing hard now. I spread the blanket out as far as my arms can stretch and hold it over my head. My blanket is now a cape and I'm ten feet off the ground gracefully flying back to the dorm. I slow down, go through the double doors into the dorm, and Hunter's standing outside his room. He gives me this uncertain look and a thumbs up, like he wants to know how it went. Our dorm mates are running up and down the hallway back and forth hustling into their rooms to watch movies or have a late-night snack. Through the zig-zag of bodies I give him a nod. *Yeah, it went well. It went great. It was a night I will never forget.* I head into my room thinking, *If that's not the definition of a wingman, then you're reading the wrong dictionary.*

Chapter 13

Saucefest

n hockey, the word "sauce" refers to a pass that goes through the air. The hockey puck literally becomes a flying saucer. In drinking, sauce refers to liquor and getting sauced means getting drunk. It's a popular term on campus, both in hockey and for the pastime—getting sauced, as in getting absolutely shitfaced.

When I first started tenth grade, I was drinking every week on Fridays and Saturdays. I became a professional at hiding it from even my closest friends. It's not like I ever had a drinking problem—I just like getting a buzz on. And frankly, keeping it hidden makes it a bit more thrilling. Every weekend, I found a different person to drink with, and if I couldn't, I drank by myself and hoped I'd run into someone else drinking. I started off with Malibu, this rum that tastes like coconut, but my tolerance for alcohol grew and my drink of choice became Bacardi white rum. Really though, I'd drink anything you gave me.

Sharing alcohol is a big deal. Getting rid of the evidence—the bottle—is like hiding a body. The trick is to drink in the shower stalls, which are connected like bathroom stalls. Two people can be in adjoining showers and pass the goods back and forth. We can never get caught, and I never slipped up. The shower's a good place to drink because of the comfort of the warm water. It's relaxing. But there's another reason I like drinking in the shower—it's the only place, along with the bathrooms, that is private from the houseparents. Simply no one in authority is allowed in the shower area. No one can prevent you from taking a swig of rum and then a swig of Coke or Pepsi. I can take swigs like that and pass the bottle and repeat again until it's all gone without even the slightest chance of being seen or barged in on.

I can leave the shower with a nice buzz going, ready to get my clothes on and hit the town—I mean village. "Town" isn't really a thing here. Wilcox has less than ten small streets and, other than the school kids and their families that live there, is home to about 400 people. So, since we're out in the sticks, you're probably wondering where we get the alcohol, right? Well, I'll tell you.

Sometimes, we have dorm outings into the city, Regina, and guys sneak away and stand outside a liquor store until someone agrees to get them the goods. Other guys get Rodney, a townie, or one of the other of-age townies, to get it for them.

Then there's this extensive undercover operation. That's how I get my rum. Because, you see, I know how everything works around here. These two guys, Jim and Simmer, somehow manage to bring a lot of alcohol on campus—so much that they have runners, so of course, I'm a runner, which is like a distributor. This way, they don't have to interact with all their customers. They charge twenty dollars for a 355-milliliter bottle of whatever kind of booze you want, and they're paying maybe nine or ten bucks for it, probably less. We runners gather sales for them, then we pick the alcohol up from them. Naturally, I'm one of their best runners. I don't know how their operation got started, but I know they're making money. And they're how I get my own personal supply, too, because they make this deal with me.

"Listen," says Jim, "you get over ten bottles sold, with all the money collected, and we'll give you a free bottle for yourself." Now I can sell the free bottle, but I don't care about making money. All that matters is I can get drunk for free. Sounds like a good deal to me! So I've been doing that twice a week.

Sophie doesn't like me drinking because when you're at boarding school, getting caught is serious. It's not grounds for expulsion, at least not the first time, but you could get a lot of hours working with the grounds crew and cleaning toilets. I promised her I'd stop drinking, and I did. I don't want to break my promise or Sophie to get in trouble with her dad. That's why I quit.

***

Anyways, it's Saturday, late afternoon, and I walk up the stairs of Fred Hill and hear 50 Cent playing from the tenth- and eleventh-grade dorms. The rapper 50 Cent is a big deal in music right now, and he's repped by Dr. Dre and Eminem. I walk into the bathroom and find boys rowdy and fired up—more than usual—so I go back to the room to tell the guys that I think some of the others have already started drinking. What's weird is, even the guys inside the dorm are laying out on the study benches in the rooms, getting sun, as others are dancing to the music. Everybody's got a red cup in their hand, and I start to get pretty fired up myself. Wow, is everybody drinking?

The promise I made to Sophie is out the window, and I grab a drink. Up until this point, I've quit cold turkey, I swear. There's no discreetness here—we're all just free-pouring whatever we want. I can tell the alcohol has taken effect with a lot of the guys, even though it's just after lunch on Saturday.

But this is no typical Saturday. It's Alpotredia Weekend, two days of class reunions for Notre Dame alumni. Former students are back on campus for their five-year, ten-year, even fifty-year reunions. The current students aren't involved in the weekend at all, other than Street Sweep. So, the week leading up to this weekend, we all had half-days of classes, then we spent the afternoons cleaning the campus. It's called Street Sweep because we literally sweep Main Street. It's not as bad as it sounds. Street Sweep is great because we're out of class, laughing and talking and drinking our Diet Pepsis and Gatorades. Horsing around while cleaning. No one's giving you any shit. Like that saying, "Many hands make light work," you'd be surprised how fast 300 guys and gals can clean up an entire campus.

A lot of people show up for Alpotredia Weekend. They come from all over the world, and even if you don't know them, if they're Hounds like you, they're family. They have that look in their eye, too, that says they'd give anything to come back to this time, this moment, that we're living in. Even though you have less than twenty dollars in your pocket and a lot of these people went on to become very successful, they'd give it all away to be a teenager again in good old Wilcox. They know what we've been doing with Street Sweep because they've done it before. They say how nice the campus looks, and that feels good, having people appreciate our hard work, as past Hounds had thanked them during their time, I'm sure.

All these people are talking to teachers they knew from years ago who are still there, and everybody's catching up. The administration and the staff are probably busier on Alpotredia Weekend than the whole rest of the school year. There's dinners in town, and banquets...stuff like that.

And now it's making sense. Nobody really planned this, but the students figured this was the perfect opportunity to drink some Dr. Feel Good. With so many outside people on campus—I mean, the population is basically double if not more—and all the people in authority looking out for them and tending to other tasks, it's not likely somebody will notice if a student's a little drunk.

I talk to guys and girls from other dorms and smell vodka and rum on their breath. I'm surprised there are more openly drunk people than bottles I handed out the night before. I don't know how so many kids got all that liquor, because it didn't all come from me. Maybe Jim and Simmer's little business is expanding and even better than I thought. Makes sense...I am just a low-level employee paid in product.

I walk toward Kenny Hall, crushing the remaining half of my Bacardi bottle. That's right—I slam it back right in the open as the boys stare. I chuck the bottle into the garbage and keep walking. The computer lab above the gym in Kenny Hall is pretty full, but I manage to find a computer in the far back. Actually, I tell a grade-nine kid that someone in the hallway needs him, and when he stands up I hijack his seat, a common occurrence on campus.

I'm worried that my streak of not being caught is about to come to an end, and I'm saying this to Cory, who's sitting next to me. I guess I'm yelling because he tells me to shut the hell up. The computer screen is fuzzy, and I can't make anything out, so I get up and tell myself that I don't need any more of this school stuff. Some of the guys walk with me next door to the arena and a townie offers me a drink—she hands me a Bacardi with a little lime soda—and I slam it back.

The sun's setting, and if this were a movie, there'd be wolves and coyotes howling at the rising moon, but the only howling I hear is from my crazy schoolmates running wild. I hear howling near Canada Park and stumble closer until I find Laser, who's drunker than anyone I've come across all day. I've never supplied Laser or his friends with anything, so I have no clue how everyone got their liquor. All over, guys are screaming; girls are play-wrestling and singing. Everyone is having a blast. This is wonderful.

Jake Whiter is one of the houseparents in Fred Hill, and I've learned that this guy doesn't have much of a bite, but he can really bark. Jake walks past Canada Park and shouts that there's a dorm meeting. He's not my houseparent, so it's kind of odd that he's instructing all of us to get our asses inside. Nothing about this day is normal. I have a brief moment of clarity and see other houseparents scooping up their respective students. So, we boys (who are still behaving like animals) from both floors of Fred Hill have to meet in the bottom lounge.

Jake storms in and gives a speech about how being a man means having the balls to come clean. He wants us to confess. Another houseparent, John Woodsmere, stands behind him with his arms crossed the whole time. Just as Jake is about to launch into another tirade, two of my closest buddies stumble in. Skip and Cory barge in like runaway train cars. I'm screwed, I think, because they're some of my best buddies— Jake and John will undoubtedly think I have something to do with their drinking. I know we're all about to get busted, even Myles Sandler, one of my closest friends who's trying to mask the smell of vodka with ketchup-flavored potato chips. One by one, we get called into the houseparents' office and they try to get each person to spill the beans, but I don't feel like confessing yet. I'm relaxed.

So now we're having a dorm meeting right here in the lounge and everyone from both floors is here. Myles is still munching on those chips and he's starting to freak out. "Can you smell my breath?" he asks, leaning in, and I'm thinking, Jesus this guy is screwed—he's becoming his own worst enemy and he's going to get caught. "I don't smell a thing man—you're gravy." In all honesty, his breath smells like a rundown bottle depot.

No one's talking, so then Whiter backs up and says, "Okay, so which one of you is going to be a man and have the balls to come into my office and confess?"

Two guys get up—the two guys I've been drinking with. They follow Jake into the houseparents' office and I know I'm done for.

I'm still playing it cool, because I've dealt with this whole "What have you been drinking?" accusation before. But now more people are getting up and walking down the hall, and I'm thinking someone's going to point the finger at me. After all, I'm a known shit-disturber. These guys who are confessing are never in trouble, ever. I just sit there with my mouth shut and eventually I get called into the office. Jake gets right in my face.

"Listen here, you little shit, because I'm only going to ask you this one time. Tell me what that smell is on your breath right now." I stand my ground, and Jake slaps his hand on the chair.

"Christos, this isn't a joke. You're going to be in a lot of trouble, and the longer you wait to tell us, the bigger punishment you'll get." I have a bad feeling that more than 90 percent of those involved have confessed already. I smirk and keep denying it over and over again.

"Oooookay," I finally say, "I'll tell you what the smell is." I lean back in the chair, pretty smashed.

"Good. Tell us now so we can all go to sleep!"

"The smell on my breath," I say, cue the pause for dramatic effect, "it's Heinz 57."

"Get the hell out of here!" Whiter yells at the top of his lungs. "Smartass! Jerk! Prick!"

I walk out the door, and he's still calling me names, but I can't hear the rest of them 'cause I'm down the hallway and he's fading away.

Later, I write some bullshit confession on paper. This is some kind of protocol thing that eliminates the school's responsibility for any wrongdoing. It's also mandatory for them to dish hours. I don't care about the confession—it's my first time getting caught, and I'm not the only one in trouble. All my friends are getting hours too, so why not me?

* * *

The next morning, I find out that because of our drinking, the most hours in the history of the school are being dished out. Everyone's just laughing about it—it's legendary! We're talking about something like 120–180 kids getting busted for drinking.

Even John smirks. "Yeah, you guys just had a giant saucefest."

But now we have to call our parents and tell them what we did. Skip's the most nervous because his dad can be a real hardass.

I can't help him with his dad, but I can make his hours easier. Lucky for him, I've gotten in plenty of trouble before and I know which jobs around campus are easiest for getting these hours done. The key is to go to the staff members who don't want you around or those who are really nice. You just don't want to go to anybody who's not cheerful and looking to make everyone else miserable. Like, if you do hours in Varsity and get stuck with Whiskers—who obviously hates his job—he's going to bust your ass for an hour and a half and only give you credit for thirty minutes toward your hours list. But, if you go to Lily Tamsker, the free-spirited art teacher—and yeah, the mom of the townie who gets kids alcohol—you might do thirty minutes of work and she'll give you five hours. Seriously, this happens often.

"Don't worry, I got this," I tell Skip. "C'mon. Let's go to the art room."

Lily's really sweet and easy to talk to. I walk up to her and smile. "Lily," I say, "we got into a little trouble and figured: what better place to come help out but the art room, since you're my favorite teacher."

She gives us work to do, and we spend maybe an hour and a half cleaning trays and brushes. Lily gives us each ten hours on our sheets—nearly a third of the requirement. We head out the door and we're laughing all the way back to the dorm. Inside, guys are washing walls, cleaning toilets, and vacuuming the floors like a bunch of suckers. The houseparents are clearly loving every minute of this. Back at the dorm, I find Subz in the bathroom and he asks me how I can be in such a good mood after we all got hit with hours. I show him my doc sheet with ten hours done and he completely loses it. He starts screaming in the mirror as I stand there laughing.

"Listen man," I tell him, "come to Varsity with me and I'll get you some free hours marked off." He grabs his stuff, and we walk out of Fred Hill.

In Varsity, they'll give you some stuff to do, but eventually, you'll just get in their way.

"It'll be perfect," I tell Subz. "You'll get five or six hours ticked off for an hour of work."

Garth, a short bald man with round glasses is on duty in Varsity. He always pretends he doesn't like me, but since I've worked so many hours under his care this year, I think he's warming up to me.

"What did you guys do now?" he snarls at me and Subz. I explain that we'd simply had some social cocktails, and everyone had been over-the-top dramatic about it. He signals us to the back of the kitchen to do some light work, like throwing out the garbage and changing the trash bags. After twenty-five minutes of work, he marks off five hours on my and Subz's sheets and tells us to get the hell out of there. On my first morning of punishment, in less than two hours, I've already ticked off fifteen hours of work.

I get a lot of joy out of scheming the system. Maybe that's why I continue to challenge it. I had some harmless fun, got a good buzz on, and helped out my buddy Subz. And now I can claim the title of being one of the guys responsible for the most hours dished out in the history of Notre Dame. It doesn't get much better than that.

Chapter 14

Liquid Courage

at Stevens, Rod Stewart, Sheryl Crow... They all had it right. The first cut *is* the deepest. My lady friend and I end it over the summer. It sucks, but I'm headed back to school in Saskatchewan and to the guys at Notre Dame.

I'm in eleventh grade, but it's going to be different without Sophie. All the older kids I looked up to last year graduated, and even the eleventh- and twelfth-graders aren't all coming back. They're staying back at home for their last school years. Even Hunter is doing his senior year at his local high school in Vancouver. These people have been a part of my life on campus for a long time, and I can't imagine getting through eleventh grade without them. It's a hard pill for me to swallow, and I need to find something to fill the void. I'm thinking about this at the end of the summer, and it doesn't take me long to come up with a plan.

Most of that summer, I worked at my family's restaurant where we sell food like pizza, wings, lasagna, subs, and the famous *donair*, or what most people refer to as the gyro—that stuff is so much better than the prison slop we get in Varsity. I got to eat the food, but the main reason I worked there was to hang out with my brother. He's been there since graduating from high school, and I find him much cooler than myself. He's always looking for a side hustle, and like me, he kind of gets a kick out of seeing what he can get away with. So when I tell him about the illicit alcohol distribution system at school and the crazy money kids pay for booze, he's all ears.

You can't have liquor on campus. We're all underage kids, and if you get caught, it's serious. Remember saucefest and all the hours we got? It's like that, but usually worse when you get caught drinking by yourself. Since liquor's hard to get, you know everybody wants it—and, as I'd learned last year, they'll pay.

Simmer and Jim—the guys who ran the business—have graduated. So other than the townies and the random student who brings in maybe a few bottles at a time, there's no competition or organized system. My brother and I spend the rest of the summer scheming, because there's a lot to figure out, like what size bottles to sell, how much to charge, and most importantly, how to get it into campus

Here's the really cool part that's going to let us get it on campus with nobody noticing: we're not using liquor bottles. Instead, we're using clear water bottles. Jim and Simmer were selling whiskey and dark run, but we're buying only vodka and white rum, so it looks just like water in those plastic bottles. We put a little dot on the bottom to tell them apart—red for vodka, black for rum—so we don't have to open them up and risk getting caught by the smell. That would ruin the whole operation—plus, I don't want any spillage. My brother's going to screw the caps back on perfectly, so you can't even tell the seal's broken. Twenty bucks is standard for a 355-milliliter "Mickey," but we want to sell more volume, so we go with 500-milliliter bottles at thirty-five dollars a pop.

I'm back at school now, and I can't believe it. Last year, I drank for fun, but now I'm in the bootlegging business. We have everything planned, just like clockwork. I even told my brother how to pack it and ship it so we won't get caught. By now, in my third year, I consider myself an expert on the houseparents' and teachers' routines. I know the best and worst times to pick up a parcel from Maynard House, the students' mail center. Lunchtime is perfect because everybody's at Varsity eating or back in the dorm goofing off before classes start. The sidewalks are empty, and you have less of a chance of suspicious eyes looking at you.

I position myself with a view of Varsity, wait for the second group of students to head in, and make my move. The students naturally block the door so no teachers can get a good look at me as I walk by, headed for Maynard. This might sound a little excessive and paranoid, but I seem to attract unwanted attention no matter what I do. So now I'm in the mail center, looking at all the boxes in the foyer that are waiting to be picked up. You can't just take a package, even if it has your name on it. You have to sign for it first, or you could get hours. So I check the log to see if my delivery has arrived, and not only is it here, there's a second package from my mom. Delightful.

Then I head back into the foyer to locate my special delivery, and I can't believe what I see: my brother didn't pack the bottles like I told him at all. He lined them up on a cardboard flat, covered the top with an upside-down cardboard flat, and Saran-wrapped the whole thing. The bottles of vodka and rum are right there in plain sight for anybody to see!

It's all visible: the blue screw tops and "President's Choice" label, which is the cheapest water you can buy, except these bottles are filled with my million-dollar idea. I'm so scared that someone's going to figure out what I'm up to, I don't want to go near those bottles. I stand there, debating, not knowing what to do.

Then I find my mom's care package. I know what's in it because she always sends my favorite stuff. Beef jerky, Old Dutch Bar-B-Q potato chips, Dad's Oatmeal Goodie Rings, Little Debbie Cookie Creme Cakes, plus licorice for Christian. She always sent something for Christian, and his mom sends me stuff too. Mom sends me a care package every week, pretty much.

I take that love-filled care package and drop it right on top of Lucifer's liquid. Then I pick the whole thing up and back into the door, swinging it open with my back because my hands are full. Ned Cushman's standing there; I practically walk right into him. Ned's one of the Christian Ethics teachers, and probably the most wholesome person on campus. He's always cheerful and eager to help.

"Holy cow, Christos," he chuckles. "Let me give you a hand with that!"

"Oh, no," I mutter nervously, "I got it." *Jesus, I haven't even sold a bottle yet, and I'm busted already.* Ned's got a firm grasp on this package of bottled booze, all plastic-wrapped between sheets of cardboard, and there's nothing I can do. If I resist at all, I'm going to look suspicious, so I let him take it. My stomach's in knots now, and me and Ned are walking toward the dorms. Lots of guys and even some of the girls across campus know about my operation. I had to tell them, so I'd have clients lined up as soon as this first shipment came in. They all knew I had booze coming in the mail.

They see me walking with Ned, who is now carrying all of the bottles and some people stop in their tracks and stare in disbelief. Keep in mind that this is a good three-minute walk, and with the package being so heavy, more like five minutes. I have to keep up the chit-chat with him for a while. Ned asks me why my mom is sending me water and I just shrug and say, "Oh you know, Mom knows best!" As scared as I am, I have to stay calm or at least pretend I'm calm.

My body wants to freeze. I keep moving, trying not to seem suspicious by stuttering or looking nervous. I have to stay sharp and relax. Finally, he lays my package on my desk while other dorm mates try to hide their disbelief as they process what's happening, and so do I. The Christian Ethics teacher just helped me smuggle alcohol into the dorms.

Chapter 15

The Setup

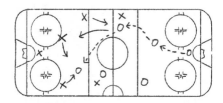

n grade eleven, my room is in the opposite wing of where I was in grade ten. Just like last year, I'm right next to the houseparents' office. My room, G-2, is a four-man room designed the same way as all the others in the building.

I can already see a few possible hiding spots for my product—all that alcohol my older brother is sending me. Running an operation like this, preparation is essential. Coming into the room, the door swings right and there's a boot rack on the left. This is home, and I might be able to stash some bottles behind the boot rack. I have some other hiding places scoped out, but I'm not telling anyone where they are.

Even though it's a four-man room, there are only three of us. It's me, three-year Hound Ethan Spencer, who I lived with in Edith Hall during my grade-nine glory days, and Matt Lucas, who was on the floor above me in grade ten.

Ethan's a straight shooter. I have a feeling they put him with me and Matty hoping he'll be a good influence. I don't tell Ethan what I'm up to, and even though I like him, I don't like having to sneak around him.

Matty is my right-hand man, and we discuss things in advance. He's in charge of scooping up new clients and potential runners, and he's the main guy who meets up with customers when they need a bottle. That means I don't ever have to see customers face-to-face if I don't know them. At first, most of the bottles are already pre-sold, so Matty doesn't have much work to do until the next batch comes in. I pay him in booze or whatever he wants from the Hound Shop or Canteen. Matt's easy to work with. We are smooth sailing.

My brother's buying in volume now, which has driven the price down and our profits up. He gets these large three-liter bottles and puts the product into smaller 500-milliliter water bottles that I'm selling for thirty-five bucks. It's not just straight vodka or rum, either. After all, this is business. He's filling the water bottles up with liquor to about 300 mills and topping them off with water. This waters down the product, but it increases our profit margin and makes the liquor easier to swallow. It also reduces the chances of kids getting too drunk drinking straight alcohol. It's what I like to call high profit, diluted risk.

For this operation to work, I need organization, focus, and professionalism—basically, everything I've neglected in the classroom over the past two years. So I change things up right at the start of grade eleven. First off, I join the football team, and even though they never put me on the field, I never miss a practice or a game. I'm staying out of trouble in school, and I'm even doing my homework for a change. I do little things like picking up garbage on the way to Varsity to stay humble and keep a low profile instead of drawing attention to myself. I'm an entrepreneur now, and to keep the money coming in, I have to stay out of the spotlight as much as possible and keep my "storefront" looking presentable.

It's been a week since the first load was sold and there have been no problems. If a student gets caught with my alcohol, I tell him to just take the hours if they ever want the product again. The staff knows there's alcohol on campus, but frankly, they don't really seem to dig too deep into where it's coming from as long as you confess. Once they catch you, you can tell them anything: *I brought it from home. I got in on the last dorm trip to the city. I got it when I was on sick leave. I had someone in the city get it for me.* Just give them something and make it sound like you're being honest when you promise that it will never happen again. Take your hours, and everybody's happy. I mean, they were young once too, right? They know we're going to do whatever we want to do, so mostly, it's just a protocol thing to make sure we admit it came from off-campus so no one can say the school's responsible for little Johnny or Trisha getting tipsy.

Some kids even spill what little they think they know to Jake and John, but they have no evidence, and no evidence generally equates to no crime. The problem is that I feel the pressure build with every breath check and locker search. A breath check, if you don't know, is when they sniff for alcohol on your breath. When you come into the dorm at curfew on weekends, the houseparents ask you to breathe in their face and they try to smell if you've been drinking. A locker search is when everyone is sent to the dorm lounge while the houseparents and house leaders go one by one to each room to look for stuff that's not supposed to be there. If you have something stashed away in an obvious hiding spot, you're 110 percent screwed.

I know these guys, my dorm mates, well, and I can always tell who's hiding something. They always come up empty in G-2 though. How so? I'm in good with our house leaders and the house leaders in the other dorms. They'll tip me off if a locker search is about to go down. I have eyes everywhere. So many students are helping me in little ways that it's next to impossible to catch me. Helping me also is that I stopped drinking completely. I don't drink at all anymore. No matter how badly I want to, I don't touch it. Biggie Smalls, the late rap artist, may he rest in peace, said to never get high on your own supply. Sage words of advice, and I'm following them.

By the time my brother sends a second load, I have a solid network of runners and don't have to sell the stuff myself. With runners in every dorm and Matty doing the drops, my operation is running smoothly. I have rules to control every aspect too, like not selling alcohol until midday on Friday. This prevents anybody from getting drunk before Friday night. I've promised guys like Dennis Quill that I won't sell to his younger brother in grade nine. I respect that ninth-graders are small and get drunk easy. Besides, I don't want to corrupt them. I don't sell to most girls, but if a grade-eleven or -twelve girl wants something, I'll usually give it to them. I've known these girls for years, but for the most part, girls are a big "hell no." They bring drama, and with drama comes trouble, and trouble increases the likelihood of getting caught, at least this is what I think.

I do have two girls involved in the operation though: Sophie, who I want to keep close to me, and Emma Peters. Sophie and Emma hold onto the money for me. Emma's dad is the principal, Owen, and her mom is the head of residence. This may seem outrageous, but both girls are good friends of mine, so I trust them, and both have parents as staff on campus. They're also my insurance, especially Emma. Even if I get caught, how is the school going to crucify the daughter of the most important administrators? Both girls want me to stop. They say it every time I give them money to hold, and that makes me think they care about what happens to me, but I'm not going to stop, at least not yet.

Word travels fast, and my business is growing. I feel like I need to find alternative places to hide my product. I wish I could have one central place, an office of some sort to store all the bottles. Across from my room, there's a small, two-man space with two lockers. It's hot here in September, and there's no air conditioning in the dorms. Worse, there's something going on with the furnace in that room, and it's like a sauna in there, so no one's moved in yet. I think about that room because it's still unoccupied, but the only problem is, it's locked. John has the key, and he never lets his keys leave his sight.

* * *

Today's Saturday, and by some miracle, houseparent John Woodsmere has just lent his keys to my friend Abs, who's above me on the second floor. Abs is always stirring the pot, but he's also extremely punctual and detail-oriented. This makes the staff trust him. John tells him to use the keys for whatever chore he's doing and then just throw them on his office desk. I can't believe my luck. John would never lend me the keys, but Abs...

I wait by the houseparents' office and tell Abs to toss me the keys when he's done. Abs knows better than to ask questions. We're Hounds from the same kennel, so he's going to do it, but he doesn't want to know what I'm up to. This is the guy who gave me Viagra and then admitted to it to try to keep me out of trouble. He was in the ultimate hall slide—that massive water fight we had in my first year. We've been buddies since ninth grade. Abs is my guy. He gives me the keys, a big cluster of them.

"Make sure you put 'em back on John's desk," he says, "Whatever you're doing, just make sure it doesn't come back on me."

John is headed back here—I can see him through the window. I rushed to G-1, the two-man room, and try the first key. Nothing. Second key, nothing. There's a dozen keys on this thing and I can't find one that works. I fail ten times in a row, and every time somebody walks by I have to hide the keys and pretend I'm not doing anything.

Just two keys left. I push one in and it slips into the keyhole. Bingo. I push the door open, and I'm hit with a wave of hot air. I walk inside and close the door behind me, slip the room key off the keyring, and press my ear to the door. Silence, so I make a mad dash back to the houseparents' office. I throw the keys on the desk and just as I turn around, John walks through the double doors. I jog toward my room.

"What the hell are you up to?" John hollers. It's not like he saw me coming out of his office or anywhere near G-1, but people always assume I'm up to something, and rightfully so, because I am.

"Nothing, just going to grab a drink in my room," I tell him. John can smell mischief before I'm even done doing it.

I hide the key in the far corner of my bed, under the mattress pad. I'm elated. I finally have my own office, a headquarters for my business, but I can't share it with anyone. Things are looking perfect. Then a loud voice comes bellowing from the hall.

"WHOEVER HAS MY MASTER KEY, YOU HAVE THIRTY SECONDS TO GIVE IT BACK!"

Shit. I had no clue it was the master key. This is a big deal. The master key opens everything on campus, so John must be really pissed. I grab the key and pretend I'm walking to the bathroom, and when John's back is turned, I run up the stairs and place the key in Abs's room, on the shelf near his bed. I'm not trying to frame him; I just know John will go way lighter on him than he would for me. I tell myself that Abs will be fine with this. I'll just act stupid.

I run back down to my room, and a few minutes later, Abs pops in.

"Hey 'Stos, did you take the master key?"

"No man," I say. I'm lying and he probably knows it as he shakes his head at me. He heads back up to his room and he must have found the key where I left it, because I can hear him yelling to John that he found the key.

I can hear them out in the hall now, and Abs is telling John he has the key, but he didn't take it off the keyring, so he doesn't know what happened.

"Did you lend the keys to anyone else?"

"Yeah, I did, sorry, but Christos said he needed it for something," Abs says, totally unaware that he just implicated me for taking the master key. It's not like he has a choice.

John confronts me, and I deny everything, of course. This is John, the same guy who's been busting me for shit since I started here at Notre Dame. He's been on me for over two years now—since grade nine. He says that he knows when I'm lying and he knows how to get the truth out of me.

"If I don't find out who took the master key, dorm workouts every morning until someone comes forward," he says, then he screams at me, "Tell me now and you won't get punished! If you don't, I'm reporting you and you're going to get in the best shape of your life!"

What he's saying is that this is serious enough for him to get upper authorities involved. It's what houseparents do when they can't take care of a problem themselves, sort of like when there's a riot and the mayor has to call in the National Guard. I really don't want him bringing this problem to a higher authority because then the punishment will be out of his control. I know that even though John's always giving me shit, he still has a soft spot for me and doesn't want me in serious trouble with the school. It's a love/hate relationship with John, as he loves to pretend he hates me.

If John reports this and I get found out, it's one strike and I'm suspended. If I get two strikes, I'm out—basically expelled. Even though I have no actual strikes, a build-up from grades nine and ten means that I am on everyone's shit list.

Well, that's just great. I sit and mull it over for an hour or so while the boys watch *Sex and the City*, which is a popular show amongst some. I'm not focused on Carrie Bradshaw's problems though; I'm focused on mine. I'm screwed, and I know it. I don't want anyone else to get in trouble for what I've done. Finally, I walk down to John's office and tell him that I was just messing around and took the key off his keyring as a joke.

John shakes his head. "I need you to write that out and sign this document saying what you did."

"No problem," I say. I write a makeshift confession and John issues me sixteen hours for disrespect. He tells me I can start my hours at dinner. Okay, so it looks like everything's cool.

* * *

It's Sunday, and I'm sitting in Varsity laughing with the guys about the whole thing. I go to the kitchen to get a hairnet and a garbage bag so I can start my hours, and here's John in front of me. He stops me like he's got something to say.

"Christos," he says, "if it was up to me, the sixteen hours would be all you'd get."

Oh man, this isn't sounding good.

"But since you waited too long to tell me it was you who took the key, I had to report it."

Dammit. The senior staff members don't have a soft spot for me like John does. I do my hours, worried the whole time about what's going to happen. Later on, I get the news: one-day in-school suspension until they can figure out what they want to do with me next.

Everyone's at supper, and I'm looking for something to occupy my time while I think about all the trouble I'm in. I go into the bathroom opposite my dorm in Fred Hill. I'm kind of fascinated by the power and pressure of the toilets. If you put your fist in a toilet paper roll and thread the paper into the toilet, then you put your foot on the toilet lever and rotate your hand to release the paper, the toilet will suck the whole roll down. I know this because I've been flushing rolls since tenth grade. Edith Hall, my grade-nine home, was an old building with very weak water pressure. Fred Hill and Max Bell toilets though? Now these sons of bitches get serious torque. They're commercial toilets, so you don't have to wait for the water to fill the bowl before you can flush it again. It just keeps roaring. So I got my foot on the lever and I'm pushing it down, and I get the whole roll of paper down the toilet with ease. I figure it's a good time to step it up a notch and see what these things are made of. I flush a toothbrush and the same thing—*whoosh*—right down, no problem. Sandwich wrapper...gone. Chips bag? Embarrassing performance, but after a second, right down the old toilet. *Man*, I'm thinking, *this thing is powerful*. Then I go into the nearby lounge and find this green apple. Perfect.

I'm sizing up this apple, holding it up and looking at it with one eye, and the other eye closed, thinking it'll go down. But I have to know for sure. A small part of me is saying, "Do it," while another part is saying, "Do it RIGHT NOW." Why not? I put my foot on the toilet lever and let it run for a minute, then I toss the apple into the mouth of the porcelain beast. The apple disappears, but the water starts to fill the bowl. *Oh no, it's stuck,* I'm thinking. Well, that's enough entertainment for one day. I take my foot off the lever and head back to my room.

***

Monday morning, I'm told that I have to help out the maintenance guy during my suspension. I head over to the maintenance shed, and there he is, D.M.G. The M and the G are for "maintenance guy," but we call him D.M.G. for "drunk maintenance guy." He's older—probably in his sixties—kind of rugged, and wacky-looking, which makes him look like he's permanently intoxicated. He says we need to go to Fred Hill to fix a toilet. What are the odds?

He's gathering up his tools, and I notice there's a ride-on lawnmower in the front outside the building, and it's just sitting there with the motor running, with nobody on it. Of course, I hop on and start cruising. D.M.G. just loses it. He's screaming at me like a wild man, which is kind of scary. I hop off the mower.

He makes a fist and I can see his dirty thumbnail clenched over his fingers. "I should kick your ass!" Then he says, "LET'S MOVE." I follow him into the dorm and straight to the bathroom where I flushed that Granny Smith apple.

D.M.G. bends down (ass crack showing, of course) and unscrews the toilet. "Yep, happens all the time," he says, "Too much goddamn paper. You kids are so wasteful, but you're young and you like to have your fun."

I can't keep it to myself. "Can I tell you something?"

"Yeah?" he says, with a crooked smile.

"Okay, but you're not going to get mad?"

"No," he says, returning his gaze to the toilet and tilting it away from the floor.

"It was me that clogged the toilet."

He pushes the toilet aside and looks down into the hole in the floor.

"I think it was an apple that did it," I confess.

"Well then," he says, "you're going to fish it out."

I guess that's fair, and probably not even the worst punishment I've had out here. I can see the apple down in the pipe, bobbing in the water. It's bruised and brown, not like the shiny green apple from yesterday.

"Okay then," I say. "I just need some gloves."

This guy's looking at me and he just laughs with his crooked smile and off-color teeth. "No gloves," he says with a smirk. Then he points at me and says, "Use your bare hands." More laughing.

"No," I say.

"Do it!" he demands.

Now I'm scared, and I stand there, frozen. There's no one around to save me from this lunatic.

"Listen here, you little shit," he growls, and his tone is shifting from weird to all-out angry—borderline psychotic. "You may not have anything better to do today, but I do. So get your snot-covered hand down that pipe and fetch the goddamn apple."

I'm standing there trying to work up the courage to stick my hand into the narrow opening. I'm not getting out of this, I guess, so I just need to get it over with. D.M.G. is crouched down on the floor near the hole, and I pull my shirt up over my nose and lean over to get a closer look. There's the latch ring that holds the toilet to the floor, and a hole, and the pipe. The pipe where all the waste goes. The apple's not brown because it's bruised. It's actually covered in shit. This crazy bastard is cackling, and his nasty, foul-smelling breath floats up under my shirt. I get a whiff, and holy hell, it's as bad as the shitty toilet pipe.

"Do it! Do it! Do it!" he's yelling at me now, still cackling away and holding his belly.

I hold my breath, close my eyes, and grab the apple. It's slippery, but I get a hand around it and pull it out, then I open my eyes and hand the apple to D.M.G.

"Don't give it to me, you little shit!" he hollers, pulling away. "For Christ's sake, put it in the garbage."

I'm gagging, dry-heaving. I don't know if it's from the apple or D.M.G.'s breath. I throw the apple in the garbage and head for the sink. There isn't enough soap and water in the world to wash this nightmare away.

I can hear D.M.G. on his radio and apparently, there's a clog in one of the girls' dorm's toilets too. Well, I'm not responsible for that one. And since guys aren't allowed in the girl's dorms, I'm off the hook. But I'll forever wonder which girl took a "grumpy" so bad that it required a call up to maintenance.

We gather up the janitor tools and take them back to the maintenance shed. I'm so relieved I don't have to deal with this guy anymore. He's probably glad to be done with me too. I guess we've both had enough of each other.

So it's finally over, and I head back to my dorm. John is there to greet me.

"Take a seat," he says, ushering me into the houseparent's office. "Okay, so here's the deal. You're going to get two weeks of suspension. I already spoke with your mom and she said, and I quote, 'I read the books about the old days. You put his ass on the Farm.'"

What? I'm thinking, *Getting sent away for two weeks is going to be the punishment? They're not sending me home?*

John tells me they're sending me to the Farm where I'm going to have to work for two weeks. Apparently, when you get suspended, you can either go home or you can go to the Farm. The Farm is a place that the school sends kids who don't return home for suspension, either because they live overseas, or their parents just don't want to see them. My mom doesn't see sending me home as punishment. She wants the school to put me to work instead. To be honest, I'm now excited about country life.

A nice little break from school could be interesting, but I'm in need of more product, and if I'm not there to pick it up, it'll just sit there. I have people waiting for it, so I have to make arrangements. Matty can accept the parcel, so I call my brother to give him the instructions and Matty's full name so he can pick it up at Maynard House.

I also tell my brother to start putting the alcohol into smaller bottles for a reduced price. A lot of kids have been getting too drunk, too fast, and I need to tighten up the operation. It turns out that my brother thought we have seven or eight hundred kids at the school, like the high school he went to, not less than four hundred. He thought all the alcohol he was sending was going to a lot more kids, but there are just 330 kids at Notre Dame, and not all of them are buying my product. This is something we hadn't discussed before and probably should have, because putting all that alcohol out there means a lot of kids have been getting drunk, and fast.

I go back to G-2 and wait for Matty to return from Varsity. We hang out with some of the other guys, but as soon as they leave, it's all business.

"You're getting two parcels," I explain. "I'm going to be gone for two weeks, and this should keep you busy with things. You're getting one load of 500-milliliter bottles, and then a second load that's all chubbies."

Matty listens and nods, understanding.

"Chubbies are twenty dollars and the 500 mils are thirty-five dollars." The prices seem lopsided, but it's for a reason: we already built clientele, so now I plan to switch the product over to the smaller, chubby bottles in the future. The margins will go even higher.

Matty knows the system, so I don't have to worry. I tell him I'll try to call once a week. Even though we have cell phones to text each other on campus, there's no reception at the Farm. I'll use the landline if I have to call. I'm going to take my punishment and be the best me possible, with no suspicious activity. Just a hardworking country boy. Giddy up.

Chapter 16

The Farm

pack a suitcase for my two-week work trip: jeans, sweatpants, T-shirts, toiletries. Then I head over to Maynard House, the same building where my product is coming in, unbeknownst to practically everyone on campus. There I meet two of the sweetest people I've ever met in my life: Terry stands at about five foot eight and is gentle and warm from the start. His wife Eleanor stands beside him. She's a good half-foot shorter and is so sweet and happy to meet me. I'm nervous at first, but they immediately make me feel comfortable and welcome.

"Well kid, let's get going," Terry says, firmly pressing his hand on my shoulder. "There's always work to be done on the Farm."

We get into an old 1986 Chevy pickup truck and I remind myself that for these two weeks, these kind folks will be getting the best version of me. We begin our journey on Main Street and head down a gravel road I've never been on before. I hear tiny rocks bouncing off the undercarriage of this old truck as I look out the backseat window.

"Is that a junk yard?" I ask, pointing.

"Sure is," Terry replies, his hands firmly on the wheel. "All the cars and trucks in this area? That's their graveyard."

The drive seems long, but I'm not sure if that's just because the road is unpaved and bumpy. I doze off for a bit until I hear Eleanor saying, "Here she is," loud enough to wake me up. There's farming equipment to the right of the truck and, in the distance, a house that looks to be one story high—my home for the next two weeks.

Terry helps me with my bags as I step out of the truck and look at the big wooden steps leading up to the front door. This is a far cry from campus.

"It's peaceful out here, but lots to do," Terry says. Inside the house, he shows me around. "You've got your shower right here, up these steps. We've got the kitchen to the left and the living room with the satellite TV." He walks down the hall and opens a door to the left of the living room.

"Just down here is where you'll be sleeping. If you get hungry at night, help yourself to anything in the fridge," he says.

"I hope you like roast beef and potatoes," Eleanor hollers. "That's what we're having for supper."

Terry and Eleanor are so cheerful and happy. I don't understand how this is anything close to punishment. I smell herbs and lemon in the air; this is marvelous. We have a good talk at supper and they both tell me that I don't have to share with them why I'm here. I tell them that I don't mind.

"I stole a key off my houseparent's keychain as a joke and it got reported before I could return it," I explain. They ask why I took the key, and I simply say, "Oh, you know, just messing around." This is a lie. I'd taken the key to solidify storage for my booze operation. That's why I'm here now and Matty is on his own for a while, but I certainly can't tell Terry and Eleanor that. No matter how cheerful they are, they don't need to know.

At supper, I'm holding conversations with these kind folks, but I'm also familiarizing myself with the place and looking around for the landline. There's a phone mounted on the wall near my room. Perfect. I'll wait a few days to make sure the package from my brother arrives at Maynard House. Then I'll check in with Matty.

After supper, I insist on cleaning up and doing the dishes. These people are so welcoming, and I want to earn their respect. I want to earn my keep too. I want them to come back and report to the school that I'm the best suspended student they've ever hosted.

We watch some TV, and I'm amazed by how different their world is. Their lives are affected by the weather, the market, the price of certain grain. It's the opposite of what I'm accustomed to. Terry gives me a report on the price of seed and the cost of manufacturing. Then he shuts off the TV.

"Well, that's enough of that," he says. "The sun comes up pretty early. Let's get some sleep."

It's morning, and Terry's giving me fair warning that the water here isn't like the water at school. I take this as a "glass full" statement because the water in Wilcox has, well, "character," and that's putting it nicely.

I'm excited to take a shower like the ones I take back home. I slide open the curtain, turn on the shower, and hop in. Woah. I'm hit with a mix of water and something coarse that smells like blood and iron. Maybe it's sulfur, but I don't know. It's absolutely disgusting. This stuff coats my skin in a thin film, and I get out of the shower feeling dirtier than before. Hopefully, my clothes can mask this stink.

I head downstairs, and there's Terry. "Christos, can you drive a standard?" he asks.

"Oh yeah, for sure," I say. That's a lie. I don't drive anything but my family crazy. When I was fifteen, I stole my brother's '94 burgundy-colored Ford Topaz once when he was away with my dad, and I almost hit two people. My buddy was so scared he literally jumped out and barrel-rolled away from the car. But I figure, I'm older now. I can do this.

I get behind the wheel in the truck without a clue of what to do. Terry says he has some farming equipment he needs to transport with his front-end loader, basically a tractor, and I need to follow him so he has a ride back. He leaves me in the driver's seat and walks away, saying that I'm the best man to help with the job. *Big mistake*, I'm thinking.

In my flat-brimmed ballcap and Notre Dame hoodie, I fumble with the controls. I have no clue what I'm doing. After a jerky start, I get the thing moving. We head down the road toward some fields he owns. I try to take it all in: the crops, the land, the equipment. It's such a stark contrast from both my world at home and my world back in Wilcox. I'm playing an album—*Jackpot* by Chingy—that I bought a few weeks earlier in Regina, a present to myself with my profit money. It isn't long before Terry stops, gets out of the loader, and walks back toward the truck.

"Christos," he hollers, "you're getting pretty far behind me. Are you sure you know how to drive that thing?"

"Oh yeah," I lie, "I'm positive. This one's just a little bit different from the one back home. Might want to get the fluids checked." Except there isn't one back home, and he probably knows that I'm just an idiot.

Terry scratches his head and suggests we give it another shot.

"You got it," I say.

Terry drives along, and I'm behind him for a nice little while, keeping up with his pace. I move the shift around like a joystick during an arcade game match. I'm going nice and smooth, or so I think, until all of a sudden: *Screech! Boom!* The truck stops dead. I'm trying to move the shifter, but it's stuck. *Great,* I think, *I've been on the job less than five minutes and I'm already costing them money.*

I try my best to move the shifter as Terry makes his way from the loader back to the truck again. *Come on,* I tell myself, *try to make it look like nothing is wrong.* Terry's not buying it.

"Okay, young man," he says, wrapping his hand over the rolled-down window. *How can he stay calm when I'm making his job so much harder?* I wonder.

"It doesn't look like this is a good idea, so let's just get you on out of there. Jump in the loader with me. We'll get this old beast tied up and give it a drag."

"Yeah, no problem, Terry," I reply, nervously spinning my hat around. "Guess I just couldn't quite get'er figured out." I notice I'm starting to talk like Terry and his wife.

I sit in the passenger seat of the loader, roll down the window, and watch Terry in the side mirror. He gets into the truck and is trying to put it in gear, I guess, then he hollers loud enough for me to hear, "What in the hell?"

"Something wrong, Terry?" I holler back, trying to cover my guilt.

"Well, I just can't seem to get this darn shifter to move," he says.

Hopping out of the loader, I walk back toward the truck, nodding in agreement. "Yeah, I hear ya. I couldn't get'er goin' the right way either. Definitely the fluids...100 percent."

I press my heels down into the loose gravel and spin. "Well, I'll be in the loader if you need me," I say. I start to laugh nervously and lower my head so he can't see.

Terry finally manages to get the truck working so that the loader can drag it. Back in the loader, he says, "Well, that was interesting." Terry chuckles, then he tells me, "Okay, we're going to get this stuff where it needs to go, and then we're going to drop off some hay bales for the cows."

Good. That doesn't sound like something I can screw up. We get to a large, open field and Terry tells me to wait next to a smaller tractor with a forklift on it. He gets in and picks up some hay bales with it, then he motions for me to follow him on foot. After a ways, he drops the bales in the middle of the field.

Terry parks the tractor and says, "Okay, now we're gonna go around and unwrap them so the livestock can get in there and eat."

I can see the hay bales are tied up, and I guess he wants us to cut the ropes. Terry looks at me, but I don't move a muscle. I'm not sure what to do.

"You grab the string with one hand and pull it toward you. Then take your knife and cut the string." He's using his hands to demonstrate what he's explaining with his words. I just stand there in awe, squinting up at this man. He's a real-life cowboy. And if you asked me, his ruggedness, his gentle voice, his calm movements...Terry's a man's man. A hard-working provider, proud father, grandpa, get-up-at-the-crack-of-dawn whis-key-drinking farmer.

I tell him I'm ready to try. I feel incredible right now. I'm humbled that Terry's inviting me to help him out with this task, but I'm sure a quick chat with my mom or dad would have him thinking otherwise about me and my level of responsibility. He hands me a pocketknife. Clutching the blade in my gloved hand, I picture a life on the calm hills, the wind blowing past my cowboy hat, my wife down yonder, ringing a bell and calling out, "Supper's on!"

"Christos, this knife is very special," Terry explains, pulling me out of my daydream. "I've had it a very long time. It's always done good to me. I want you to use it. Just be careful."

"Wow," I say. "Of course, Terry!"

I'm cuttin' strings, tuggin' rope, and finally start to see how my contribution's adding up. As I cut the strings, Terry wraps them around his hand. "That's it," he says. "Good stuff."

Terry walks back to the tractor to toss the string in, and I just stand there, proud of myself. Feeling confident, I do some tricks with Terry's special knife, tossing it back and forth in my hands and throwing it up the air. But now my hands are empty. The knife's gone, and I have nothing to cut the strings with.

I reach my hand into a bale of hay hoping to find the knife, but it's gone, buried deep in the hay. I have to tell Terry what happened, and he helps me comb through the hay straws with both hands. *Dear God, please let us find this knife.*

After about five minutes of searching, Terry rubs his sleeves over his face. His calm exterior turns to a certain look that scares me far more than any yell could. Between his heavy, frustrated breath and the cool October wind, I'm frozen in my tracks.

"Just get in the truck, Christos." I oblige. What else is there to do? First, I messed up the truck, and now I've lost the special knife. I have no clue what he'll possibly have me do next. For the rest of the day, Terry doesn't have me do anything. I sit in the truck and watch him and his son-in-law Trevor manage fuel tanks. I suppose it's for the best.

Eleanor drives up after a while and joins them for a laugh, with Terry waving his hands back and forth. I know they're probably talking about me and I deserve it. This isn't what I want for these two weeks. Eleanor walks up to the truck.

"Christos," she says, "how do you feel about coming back to the house and helping me in the kitchen?" This was beyond perfect. With Greek parents, I'm used to shining in this department.

Back at the house with Eleanor, I peel vegetables, season the food, and even wipe down the counters and set the table. I'm a big help, and Eleanor thanks me. She even compliments me.

I show her the way I've learned to cut onions and explain why they're cut that way. She tells me she's impressed with how much I know in the kitchen at my age. Even though she's a grown woman, this is the first time she's seen some of the things I'm showing her.

More confident now, I take control of supper, putting tin foil on the casserole dish and reminding Eleanor to set the timer. My charm is working.

"Hey Eleanor, would it be okay if I gave my mom a call tomorrow?" I ask.

"You're free to use the phone whenever you like," she replies with a smile. *Excellent. I can get ahold of Matty soon.* There's a payphone in the stairwell in our dorm, and I have the number written in my student planner.

Once dinner is in the oven, Eleanor and I sit down in the living room and chat about our lives. We spend hours talking before Terry comes home for supper, and I'm surprised how easy it is to talk to her. Our lives are so different, but we find each other opening up about our families and interests. When Terry arrives, he looks at me right away. I'm still embarrassed about earlier. He takes his gloves and coat off and simply says, "The Farm life isn't for everyone," then smiles and adds, "Let's see how you did with dinner."

Terry has a way of making me feel good about myself despite my failed attempt as a farmhand. He's pleased with supper, and Eleanor talks me up the whole time.

"It was all Christos," she says. "He did a fabulous job."

After supper, we sit around and talk more. I tell them how I love Notre Dame, especially my friends, and I conveniently leave out any details of my alcohol operation.

"What time will we be getting up for work tomorrow?" I ask.

"Me and Eleanor have to meet with some farmers not far from here," Terry explains. "We'll come back during the afternoon to get you for some work that I think you're really gonna like." He tells me I can sleep in and they'll leave a number by the phone that I can reach them at in case I need anything. *My chance is coming.*

I get up around the same time as these lovely people so we can all eat breakfast together.

"I'm going to work on some school stuff while you're away," I assure them. I set up my books in the kitchen and sit down as though I have the intention of studying. Once the truck leaves the property around 9:30 a.m., it's go time. I have to wait till eleven though, when lunch break starts. The time passes slowly, and I decide to actually try to get some homework done. When the time comes to call Matty, I look around the house, paranoid that someone will hear me talk about the operation.

I look out the window one more time. The coast is clear, and I make the call. A young male voice answers the phone and I tell him I need to speak to Matt Lucas. Whoever answers knows it's me and wastes no time. They tell me to hold on and the nerves set in, and I'm tapping my fingers in anticipation. Just when the person gets back on the line to tell me Matty will be there to talk in a few minutes, I look out the window and see Eleanor and Terry's truck pulling up onto the property.

"I'll call you later," I say, hanging up the phone. I sit back down at the table just as the doors open.

"Did you get any work done?" Terry asks with a smile. His voice sounds like he genuinely cares. That makes me feel good.

"Actually, yeah," I reply. I'm too good at this lying thing. I didn't do hardly anything at all except try to check in with Matty.

Terry tells me about our next job. "We're herding cows today, Christos, and I think you're going to like it."

I have a confused look on my face, and he says, "We're not getting out of the truck. We're just pushing the herd to come back where we need them to be."

This sounds kind of funny and not too hard, but it's much more than I bargained for. We drive back out to the fields where they have probably two or three hundred cows and the sight is simply amazing. I feel like a photographer for *National Geographic*. The view is breathtaking, like nothing I've ever seen before. In Wilcox, you can see for miles around you because it's just farmland. Here, I can see rolling hills in the distance. Clouds hover over them, and the hills rise up and seem almost to touch them. This is a rare sight to see in Saskatchewan, so I try to take it in.

Some of Eleanor and Terry's extended family members show up to help bring the cows up from the pasture. Trevor's here again, this time with his wife, and Terry and Eleanor are in another truck with me and their granddaughter Leticia, a girl who's no older than six. She has rubber boots on and her fists are clenched, which seems cute until she starts yelling out the window. I feel like I'm in a real-life Western movie. It's funny, then I realize this is actually work. Leticia gets out of the truck and I follow her, but now I'm nervous. She's just a small girl, but it turns out these giant cows are no match for her. She takes control and motions them in specific directions, and to my amazement, they follow. I'm seventeen and she's six, and she's managing these cows like nobody's business while I'm just trying to keep up. I'm a bit embarrassed. It takes all day to get these animals where they need to go, and we don't get back to the house until just before supper. Eleanor has slow-roasted a chicken throughout the day, and I sit at supper thinking that

I can't believe how much they get done on a daily basis. When night comes around, my body is aching from the endless turning that I had to do out there when the cows were moving in the wrong direction. I'm so tired and sore that I don't even want to watch TV. With Terry's permission, I'm heading right to bed.

He says to me, "You did some good work today. Sleep in tomorrow morning. I've got some things to do, but then I'll come back and get you in the afternoon."

"Are you sure?" I ask, and he says, "Yeah, don't worry about it." Terry must know how worn out I am.

I sleep in till eleven o'clock. There's a plate for me on the counter—breakfast. I call out for Terry and Eleanor, but there's no response. I open the front door and see Eleanor down at the end of the road, on the other side of the property.

She's raking dirt and she waves to me. "Go ahead and eat the food on the table," she yells. "Terry should be back shortly from where we harvest the crops." I thank her and go back inside, thinking that this is my chance. I've been here for a few days and still haven't talked to Matty. I grab the phone and keep my eyes on the window. Eleanor's still in the same spot, raking.

I can't believe it, but Matty actually answers the phone. "I can't talk long," I say, between bites and glances out the window.

Damn, this home-cooked food is so delicious compared to the stuff at Varsity. "How's business?"

"Good," Matty says. "We're down to about twelve five-hundreds and eight chubbies. Should have it moved by the time you get back." I ask Matty why the 500 mill bottles aren't selling as well, and he explains that the runners prefer the smaller bottles as they're twenty dollars and easier to hide. That makes sense, so I'm going to go forward with my plan to switch over to small bottles. It sounds like things are going smoothly from what Matty's telling me, so I feel more at ease. I tell him about my time on the Farm and how I've been working hard and doing odd jobs and staying in character. It's not that I'm not being myself, but more that I'm trying to be a better version of myself.

In about a week, I'm going to be back on campus for my hearing about my behavior, but I try to push that thought out of my head.

The next few days at the Farm are a blur. We go to Carlisle, a small town, to visit some family. We go to a trade show where I get an Oreo Blizzard from Dairy Queen. This is pretty special for someone who's used to dining hall food. It's the fall, harvest time, so Terry has me running around with him a lot. The more I learn about Terry, the more I admire him. He says that working out in God's country and on his land is peaceful and honorable work. He tells me that farmers are the foundation of society because they grow things people need every day. Thinking deeply about it, I agree.

Toward the end of my stay, Terry lets me ride in a John Deere 8600, a gorgeous tractor with an iconic lush green and yellow trim. He tells me that I can use the portable CD player in the back seat. I wish he had told me sooner so I could have known to bring my own music, but I settle for whatever CD he has in there. It's George Jones. I listen through the old muff-style headphones. The fiddle starts playing and an acoustic guitar joins in, then the lyrics begin. I've never met George Jones, but I'm convinced he wrote this song for me. He's singing about my life, my choices, and my mistakes. There's something about this moment. Sun setting, Terry plowing through the crops in front of me, George Jones teaching me where I went wrong.

These lyrics tell the story of why I'm here at the Farm. I listen to the song over and over until the batteries die. I decide that I have to talk to Matty one last time before returning to school.

It's morning, and at breakfast, I pretend I'm not feeling well so Terry and Eleanor will go easy on me. They don't seem to be bothered by the idea of me not working. I tell them that I'll try to get extra rest and catch up on homework.

"It's no problem at all," says Terry, and Eleanor adds, "We'll have sandwiches for lunch."

"Sounds good," I say softly. "Thanks." Once they leave, I wait until Notre Dame's lunch break and call Matty. I eventually get him on the phone. He says the big bottles are still selling slowly, but we need another order of the smaller guys. I tell him that we'll work out the kinks when I get back, and he shares that they haven't done a locker check since I've left.

They must think I'm the only supplier on campus. Why else haven't they done a locker check? My operation may be the largest, but a lot of townies like Tyler Miller sell product too. I hang up with Matty and immediately call my brother and tell him to just send a full flat of chubbies. We'll sell them all at twenty-five dollars apiece and make more profit. If we keep going at this rate, I won't need to work all summer and we'll still have some spending money for the next school year. Working on the Farm for a few more days, I remind myself to stay humble. Once I get back to campus, it's go time.

Chapter 17

When It Rains, It Pours

'm back from the Farm, and with my room right next to the houseparents' office, they're keeping a close eye on me. Even though the staff hasn't actually pinned anything on me, I can feel the heat. They even have on-duty staff that isn't on the regular schedule. It's getting to be too much. I'm getting locker-searched almost every day. One time John even pulls a bottle of Febreze out of my locker and says, "Is this where you're putting it?" and I'm like, "Putting what?" but I know what he means. That gets my attention, and I'm thinking maybe I better stop. I just have to sell the rest of the alcohol, pay my brother, and end the whole operation.

I'm not feeling so good, and I have a sick run, which is when you're sick and you have to go to Regina to see the doctor. Faith Peters, the principal's wife, takes me. This is not common.

On the drive to the city, she gets this serious tone and says, "Whatever you're doing, Christos, you need to stop it." I don't say anything, but I'm thinking about how her daughter Emma is holding money for me. She wouldn't say anything to her parents about what I'm doing, but I imagine a lot of other kids are talking. They can't keep quiet about anything, especially the school's biggest troublemaker selling alcohol on campus. So maybe Faith knows and maybe she doesn't. Either way, I need to stop because this is getting to me.

* * *

It's the next day, and Faith's husband, the principal, Owen, barges into our dorm room. Owen's the guy who grabbed Torch after the food fight. He's a beast of a man, and he's not looking happy.

"Whatever you kingpins are up to, stop," he bellows at me and Matty. "I don't know what you're up to, but it's got to stop." Owen and Faith are like second parents to me. I get the feeling he's trying to warn us that the situation is getting out of control and it's out of his hands. Like if something goes down, he won't be able to do anything about it. And he's the principal.

Me and Matty laugh about it, but really, inside, I'm worried. I need to get rid of the alcohol, but I can't just dump it. I still owe my brother his cut. But I'm being watched, so I can't just sell it all over campus either. I find Mason Hallso, who's a first-year student from Winnipeg and my best runner, probably because he sells to everyone. I don't sell to the girls, the younger guys, the kids from Asia, or the Europeans because a lot of them are smaller and don't know a lot about alcohol. I'm always afraid they'll drink more than they can handle and that would be terrible. Hallso knows this—especially my rule about not selling to ninth-graders. I don't want that on my conscience. But he's a good runner and my best bet for getting rid of the alcohol.

***

It's Wednesday, and I tell Hallso to meet me in the upstairs lounge of Fred Hill after lights out. Later that night, I dump my books and folders out of my backpack and ask Matty if I can borrow his camera, but I don't say why. Matty doesn't know about the hiding spot. Nobody knows about this one.

As soon as you enter any four-man room, there's a shelf on the left that's waist-high with six square cubby holes. We stick everything in there that we don't want on the floor. There are no backs to the cubbies, and you can stick your hand between them and the wall. The bottom part of this cubby hole structure is under the bed, and it's hollow.

This is where I'm stashing the liquor, and it's hands down the best hiding spot in the history of Notre Dame. There's just enough space in there to push the bottles to the back, so I push them all the way back until they hit the wall. I have to use a wire coat hanger to fish them out because I can't reach them when they're all the way in there. It's so dark that you can't even see the bottles—I use a camera to take pictures, so I know where they are. No one would ever think to look under there, and even if they did, they would never see the bottles. It's brilliant.

I use Matty's camera to locate the bottles of vodka and rum. This is the rest of my stash, and I want it gone. I load up my empty backpack, and it's so full it looks like the zipper's about to burst open. By now it's after midnight. I head up to the Max Bell lounge on the upstairs floor in the Gunner dorm. There's a guy in the hallway I know who lives on this floor. I trust him, and I talked to him earlier in the day about being a lookout for me. He's going to signal if anyone comes so I can hide the pack. Hallso's sitting there on the couch. I sit down across from him and we keep the lights off and the door closed. I whisper the plan to him.

First, me and Hallso talk for a while about the Halloween dance on Friday. I don't want to sell any alcohol at the dance because it's too risky, or even before the dance, because the kids would get rowdy and start slurring their words and somebody would figure out what was going on. I want the students to have fun at the dance, not just get drunk. And I don't want to bring attention to my operation.

At this point, I want to get out of the business. Hallso doesn't have the heat on him like I do, and I have a plan. I'll front him all the bottles I have left—everything in the pack—at cost. This isn't about making money anymore—it's about ridding myself of everything to do with the operation. I'm being watched and I know it, and it's just a matter of time before this blows up in my face. I already have one strike against me with that master key incident. I can't afford another one. I'm telling Hallso how this is going to go down, and I can't tell if he's really listening. I give him the pack and wish him luck, then I head back to my room. I'm tired, and unsettled, and worried. I just want to be done with the whole business.

***

Friday morning is another regular day on campus, but I'm feeling a lot better. The bottles are out of my hands, and that's a huge relief. Everything's cool at first, but later on, kids are coming up to me and asking for alcohol for the dance, which is less than four hours away. I tell them I don't have anything, and that I don't know what they're talking about. Then I go over to the arena to watch some hockey and try to relax. Something's not right though—there are kids here that are visibly drunk. I track down Hallso to see if he knows anything.

"How many bottles do you have left?" I ask him.

He smiles. "I sold them all," he says and tries to pass me a stack of cash like he's proud and I should be proud too. My jaw drops to the floor.

"No man, put it away!" I tell him. I can't believe he did exactly what I told him not to do. I go back to the rink and Tyler Miller is there, the townie who also sells alcohol. Tyler's a friend of mine, and I tell him what's going on and that he shouldn't sell any liquor today because everybody's already getting drunk and the dance is in just a couple of hours. Tyler looks at me like I'm some kind of an asshole. He's probably thinking, *Why should you be the only one making money around here?*

Now everything's unraveling right in front of me like a bad movie. I sit by myself in the stands, but I can't focus on the game. I'm too busy watching the disaster I created. I don't even want to go to the dance anymore, but I have to. If I don't, people will start to wonder where I am and that will just create more suspicion. Even now, in the arena, it's becoming impossible to blend in because I'm one of the few sober people here. I decide to head over to Varsity, where the dance is starting. There, I find the exact opposite of what I'm hoping for. Kids are pushing each other and causing a scene. Any houseparent or teacher around with half a brain would be able to tell that these kids have gotten a hold of some alcohol. I hang out though, but the next couple of hours are a blur. Too many kids are way too drunk, and even though I haven't touched a drop, my stomach's in knots.

I try to act as ordinary as possible, but it's not easy. I stay until the end and help the staff put away the chairs and tables, then I head over to Fred Hill's shoe room, where all the drink machines are. Every single machine has an out-of-order sign. I dig a coin out of my pocket and slip it into a slot, praying the machine eats my money. If it does, the machines really are busted. But if it doesn't, and a soda drops out, that means the houseparents are setting up a sting to catch people drinking. They don't want kids drinking soda to hide the smell, and shutting down the machines prevents everybody from getting a drink. They know we drink caffeinated stuff to try and sober up too. I press the button for a Coca-Cola and the pop can hits the bottom retrieval slot like a judge's gavel hitting its wooden plate. *Here we go*, I'm thinking, and I don't even bother with the can or the change. Instead, I tear all the signs off the machines, then I run through the dorm, both sides up and down, going in every room to tell people what's up.

I tell everybody the machines are working and to drink some pop or eat something, whatever they can find. Even water or Powerade if they have it. If they've been drinking, they have to sober up. I honestly couldn't care less if anyone gets caught. My main and only concern is people telling where they got their supply. I know it's impossible to prove that it came from me and nobody actually bought it directly from me, but I'm still worried. Making the rounds, Kip Jackson, a house leader who's a grade above me and an all-around solid guy, stops me in the hallway. He looks real upset, and he wants to talk to me in private. Of course I'll help, so we head into the lounge. It's the same room where I met with Hallso the night before to give him my stash, and I get an eerie feeling sitting there.

I'm not sure what I'm expecting, but certainly not Kip sharing his relationship problems with me, which is exactly what he's doing. He's telling me about the girl he's seeing back home in another part of Saskatchewan and how he doesn't know what to do about her, because I guess they're having problems, and I do my best to comfort him.

"No matter what happens, you'll still have this place and your boys to cheer you up, man," I tell him with conviction in my voice.

"You're a great guy," Kip says, and he's starting to cry. We both head back downstairs. I'm in my room, and there's John and some other houseparents. *Oh man, I just got set up. Kip wasn't crying over some girl—he was just distracting me so the staff could search my room.*

John looks right at me and says to the other house leaders, "You know what you're looking for, right boys?" The house leaders and administrators have every single student out of their dorm rooms and in the link now. Not just the ones they suspect are drinking—everybody. They're searching all the dorms to find out who's dirty—who's bringing alcohol on campus. All along, I've been getting tipped off by the girl house leaders, so I know to never keep product in my room if a search is coming. They won't find anything, but they're tearing my room apart. Sawyer Collins, who's from my hometown of Fort McMurray, seems to really be enjoying himself. This isn't the first time that people from back home have stuck it to me, as I experienced the first few days of my grade-nine year. That seems like a lifetime ago compared to what's going on now. They're not finding anything, but I'm keeping a poker face. No joking or mouthing off, and no messing around. I just need to get through this.

My roommate Matty is sitting on his bed, not saying anything. They've tossed the room pretty good, and I'm thinking they might be moving on. Then John grabs Matty's day planner from the side of his bed and starts flipping through it.

"Jackpot," he says. John's got a smirk on his face and he looks right at me and laughs. Then he reads from the planner. It's a list of all the alcohol sales. Matty's kept a diary? A ledger? Of every bottle sold? All I can do is watch in horror. Everyone, including John—with Matty's day planner in hand—leaves my room, which basically now looks like a war zone. I don't bother picking anything up. I sit on my bed—no sheets, pillows, or blankets; just the cold, bare, blue mattress—thinking about that phrase "You sleep in the bed you make" and how very true it seems right now. Matty shuts out the lights. I lay on the floor on top of the clothes and whatever else was thrown on the ground during the raid. I'm physically and mentally frozen, like a stone.

"Christos?" Matty says quietly, from across the room.

"Don't worry about it, man," I reply faintly. Matty knows I won't take him down with me. It's all been my doing, my product. But Matty's day planner is a mystery to me. Why was he keeping a list? If he had to write stuff down to keep track of it, why didn't he at least cross off the transactions after he made the sales? We've never given out liquor without payment first, so there's no reason to keep track of anything. It's always been a simple, straightforward operation.

Despite the day planner, I don't think John and his crew really have anything on me, but I don't know for sure and wondering about it is killing me. The past two months are playing through my mind, and I'm trying to think if there's any way they can track the alcohol back to me. I can't sleep. I roll around on the pile of rubble, playing scenarios over and over in my head. I have no idea what's going to happen to me.

***

John's at my door. It's morning, and I feel like I've been up all night. He tells me to get dressed and that I'm not supposed to go to Assembly this morning, but to report to Maynard House in thirty minutes instead. That's all he says. I walk to the showers and let the cold water run over my body, which feels lifeless. I go through the morning routine like a zombie, brushing my teeth, throwing on my clothes. On my way to Maynard House, I take a sharp left and go into the boot room first. I can hear the wind whispering outside the double doors. It's quiet now, no voices, no peers around, just me in an empty building with an empty stomach. Outside, it's cold and snowing hard, and it's cold in here too. I take a deep breath and shove all the shoes off the top rack, creating a mess of sneakers, boots, cleats, and shower sandals. I clasp my hands together, lean my elbows on the blue shelf, and rest my head on my knuckles. I won't tell you I'm religious, but I figure if there is a God, he's the only one who can help me at this point.

Outside, I bow my head again, this time against the cold and wind. Holding back tears, I walk to Maynard House. I've walked this path hundreds of times, but it seems to take a lifetime today. Slowly, I make my way up the steps. I don't want to go in, but I have to. Once inside, I twist the cold doorknob and push open the door into the meeting area. People are sitting at this round wooden table. Hallso's over there on the couch. I look at him, trying to get some clue of what's happening, but his head is down.

"Just take a seat, Christos." I don't even know who says this because I'm still looking at Hallso.

I may be a lot of things, but a snitch isn't one of them. If you're going down, there's no sense in taking anyone else with you, especially your friends. I guess I expect everybody else to be this way, especially my friends. I sit beside Hallso on the sofa, not looking at him. Now I know why I am here.

It's so quiet in that room. Then Hallso whispers, "Man, I was going to give you the money back, I swear...."

With every ounce of my being, I want to choke this kid to death. He pretended he was my friend, but he just pushed me into the fire. If I had gas, I'd dump it all over him.

Chapter 18

The Situation Room

'm looking across the table and it's full of empty faces. No smiles, no "Hey, Christos, how are you?" No emotion at all. There's no chance I'm talking my way out of this one. John's the only one standing, and he tells me and Hallso to take a seat at the table. I sit with Hallso to my right. John puts a few empty seats to my left, then sits down, like he doesn't want to be affiliated with me and Hallso at all. Mostly me, I guess. Owen is to the left of John, then Sandra Inco, Jake Whiter, Ted Mueller... All the houseparents are here, plus a few teachers. It's a table full of pissed-off, fed-up Notre Dame staff that clearly wants to get to the bottom of this embarrassment. I've outwitted, outmaneuvered, and outsmarted them all while being drastically outnumbered.

Owen, the principal, looks at me. He's got his hands clasped together on the table and he places them over his lips and begins.

"Christos, I'm only going to ask you this once. Have you been selling alcohol on this campus?"

I'm staring down at the worn-out old tabletop. I lift my head. I'm defeated. "Yes." I just want to be honest at this point. The funny thing is, I've never actually been caught with alcohol, neither with an open can nor with bottles in my room. And I've never considered confessing at all, but now the words are coming out of my mouth, and I'm not just confessing, I'm telling them about my whole operation.

I start talking, and everyone is just staring at me in disbelief. They know me, and they're probably all thinking the same thing: *Why is he confessing?* This isn't like me at all. The truth is, I just don't want to do this anymore. It's draining: the hiding, the sneaking around. It feels like I've been living a double life for the last two months. I'm telling them everything, feeling like it's the right thing to do, but another part of me is telling me that I'm overreacting and becoming my own worst enemy. Maybe I didn't have to say anything at all. But I'm here now, and I'm talking, and I keep talking.

Owen tells me to leave the room and wait for him in Abe's office. Abe's the football coach and a Christian Ethics teacher. I've never been to his office, but the building's small and the only place to go is upstairs, so up I go, up the tired old steps of this ancient place. Abe's there, and I tell him Owen wants me to wait there until he calls me back down.

I'm not stupid. They want to question Hallso on his own. This isn't looking good for me. Hallso clearly snitched on me in the first place—that's the only way they would have known for sure it was me. Who knows what else he's going to say.

Abe sits quietly at his desk while I sit in a chair against the wall, rubbing my hands over my face. There's a floor vent across from me and I can hear people talking below. I'm just out of earshot to catch exactly what they're saying. I tell Abe that this chair's uncomfortable and ask him if I can move to that other one. I'm sitting there with my head low in my hands, and I can hear the conversation in the room below. The things I hear Hallso saying make me angrier than I already am.

"He forced me to buy the product from him and sell it, and he took all the money for himself," he's saying. "He told me if I didn't sell his stuff, he'd have people kick my ass."

Of course, none of this is true. Nobody has ever been forced or even pressured into buying anything. There certainly hasn't been any bullying going on in our arrangement. I try my best to keep calm, but my mind is racing. When it's time to come back into the room, they tell Hallso to wait in the hallway. Then they ask me to tell my story again, especially how it involves Hallso, in more detail. I share how I'd met with Hallso in the lounge and gave him the bottles and how he'd sold it all. I'm not snitching, because Hallso's already told them everything—even though most of what he said is a lie. I go on to explain that if they add up the amount of rum and vodka I gave him to sell, and multiply it by what we charge for it, they should find that many dollars on him. It's stashed under his bed or in the bottom right drawer under his bed, but I don't have it, because he never paid me for anything.

I hope this is enough to make them realize Hallso's lying. I go on to say that there's really nothing else he could have done with the money since we're in the middle of nowhere and all this has gone down in the past twenty-four hours. There's nowhere for him to spend it. The next thing they do is really stupid. They go into the hallway and tell Hallso he can leave. *What?* He's going back to his room, and he can move the money anywhere since nobody's watching him. It's like they all want to blame me and let Hallso off the hook.

Somebody closes the door, and then they want to hear more. I let the story unfold. It's surprising how much they don't know, and I almost enjoy teaching them. Most of them are very quiet during the meeting. I think they're just here to make sure I don't get off easily. I can tell that what I'm saying is a lot more than they imagined was going on.

I look over at Jake Whiter. He's the houseparent that tore into me after saucefest. Jake thinks he has me scared shitless. He and Owen keep asking me questions, like it's an interrogation, but I've already said enough—there's not much else to tell. I mean, I just spilled the beans on everything. I don't want to drag it on anymore. I just want to come clean.

They want to know who's giving me the alcohol and how I get it on campus.

"Typically," I tell them, "a townie, a student resident, gets the liquor and sells it to other students, or sells it to runners and they resell it. I didn't want to deal with someone else running the supply, which is usually limited, so I cleared that bottleneck by having it shipped directly onto campus." I'm hoping that if I tell them enough, they'll have some mercy on me.

"My brother ships it to me and I pick it up and distribute it to my runners." Everyone laughs at this. They think I'm lying about my brother and trying to protect my secret supplier in Wilcox. I have to repeat myself five or six times before they begin to believe me. I'm not worried about my brother because he never sent the liquor under his own name, and the worst that'll happen to him is he'll get in trouble with our parents. Doubtful I'll be getting a Christmas gift from him this year. The holidays may be a little awkward.

The more I talk, the more impressed I am with myself for pulling this off. Really, they can't prove anything. I've been selling liquor on campus for sixty-one days, and if it weren't for Hallso's big mouth, I wouldn't even be sitting here. I've had transactions in plain sight the last couple of months. I've passed bottles of "water" right in front of houseparents and teachers, and they weren't suspicious at all. The water in Wilcox isn't filtered or fancy, not by a long shot. So it's not out of the ordinary for students to carry water bottles. The clear white rum and vodka had been a perfect choice to camouflage my product. I keep confessing, telling them more and more, trying to salvage what little chance I have of softening their anger. I tell them everything: bottles, profits, what I'm selling. I go so far as to tell them that the 500 mil bottles were too big, so I started selling chubbies.

"I told my brother to send chubby bottles, which are perfect. Just enough." I tell them all my rules, too. "It's not a free-for-all. I'm selective about who gets the liquor because I want to keep order and I don't want people getting out of control. Greed is the downfall of everything, and I suppose that's why I'm here," I say.

Hallso got greedy and sold it all in one day. Had he been trying to set a record? What he did was stupid, and that was putting it lightly. Scattering the load had been an important step to not attracting attention. Why this kid opted to mess with the basics is beyond me. I don't know why he lied about how it all went down, but I have to focus on what's at stake here. Since he took the route of lying to make me look bad, I have to go with the exact opposite tactic and tell the truth about everything. I tell them more details, including how much money I'm making. At the current rate, a conservative estimate is about fifty thousand dollars a year, tax free.

Jake Whiter stops me there. "Christos," he says, "that's more than double what I make here." He doesn't believe me. Why should he? Nobody here trusts me, and I've lied to them all so many times they have no reason to believe me now. Our conversation goes on for a few hours, and they ask me questions, sometimes the same questions, over and over. Eventually, I can tell they're starting to believe me. Everything adds up, and it's not complicated. Maybe complicated to set up, but really, it's a simple operation.

Finally, Owen's wife Faith slides a coiled book in front of me. She opens it and taps her finger on the page.

"I want you to put a check mark next to the names of everyone you sold alcohol to," she says, handing me a pen.

I can't believe it. In my grade-nine year, we were taught about Père's message, and that the world today is looking for men and women who are not for sale. Yet, they're expecting me to sell out all my customers—my friends, classmates, everyone—just to save myself, apparently. I put a checkmark beside the names of all the kids that aren't from North America: mostly the Asians and the Europeans. This is where I'm lying because we didn't just sell to Asian and European students; we sold to everyone. The only reason I gave up the Asians and Europeans was that English wasn't their first language. And if you can barely speak the language, good luck getting a confession. You might get a few smiles and nods, but that's about it. And I am not about to give up my friends.

I feel bad about lying about those other guys, but I doubt if they'll get in any trouble. I'm trying to make it sound like everybody on campus gets drunk sometimes, and they're not just buying from me, and that's kind of true. The staff probably doesn't want to believe that though; they want to think they've got a tight wrap on things and there's just a few troublemakers like me on campus. But that's not the case.

This sort of reminds me of when my mom owned a convenience store and she thought that when she was on duty, nobody could actually steal from her. The truth is that theft happened all the time, regardless of who was working. You can't control every little thing.

I keep making checkmarks and this is kind of ironic, really. They're acting like if I give everybody up, I won't be in trouble—

like maybe I can stay at the school. But if I tell on everybody, what's the point? I won't have any friends left if I snitch on all of them. So I keep putting marks next to the names of guys I don't know and have never even talked to. Faith notices I'm not naming any of my friends and asks me point-blank, "Do you sell to any of your friends?" I tell her no, and if they ever did get liquor, it didn't come from me.

I'm thinking I've done enough. I've spread the blame around enough to make them question if it's just me or if there's a bigger problem they need to deal with. They finally let me leave, after I've answered all their questions, but I still don't have the answer to the only question I care about: *What's going to happen to me?*

Owen tells me to wait for him outside his office over in Carr Hall. Classes are over now, and as I walk to the principal's office, there's a bunch of staff members standing outside Maynard House now and they're talking to other teachers and staff that walk by. I'm dying to know what they're saying. My fate is in their hands, and I want to know what it is.

I see Sophie across the street. She should be angry and disappointed in me, but I hope she's not because I care about her. She's my best friend. It's cold outside and tears are running down my red face. She's trying not to look at me because she feels sorry for me. I can't talk to her now, though. She's probably already getting in shit just for being associated with me, and she's the one who's been on me to quit my operation all this time. She must think I'm a complete fool for what I've done.

I sit in the chair near the principal's office and wait patiently, every minute feeling like a year. My head hurts, but I have no desire to eat or drink anything. I feel terrible. I sit with my hands buried in my face, biting down on my uneven teeth, reflecting on everything I've done this time. I've gone from telling myself this is the worst thing I've ever done to convincing myself that it's not a big deal and they'll forgive me. I'm lying to myself, though, because there's no getting out of this one. I have nothing left to save myself. I've shown all my cards, and I'm my own worst enemy. Owen comes through the double doors and I stand up and look him in the face, trying my best to look strong and confident.

"Christos," he says, "do you believe in God?" I'm crying still, and I tell him I prayed right before I came to the meeting. Owen presses his hand on my left shoulder and says, "We found the money exactly where you said it would be, so *I* believe you're telling the truth."

My shoulders drop. "I am telling the truth," I say. "Nobody threatened Hallso, I swear." We walk the hallway for a bit and I'm sobbing kind of uncontrollably, but slowly, the tears stop, and I calm down. Owen tells me that even though I told the truth, it's not so cut and dry. I'm a guaranteed four-year, which means I'm supposed to stay all four years and graduate from Notre Dame. But because what I did was so bad, they're going to have a special meeting.

"This has never been done before," he tells me, "but you're going to pick a staff member and a student to represent you. It can't be me or Faith for obvious reasons." Owen and Faith, like I said, have been like second parents to me and we're real close. But then he tells me that if I can't find anyone, he'll do it. I don't want to put him in that position. Some of the staff might see it as favoritism. He's the principal, and I've already caused him and his wife enough grief. And they still don't even know their daughter Emma was holding the money for me and my operation the whole time.

I now have to pick two people to represent me, and we have to convince the people in that Maynard meeting that I'm being truthful. They don't all believe what I told them about my operation, and I guess it does seem kind of ridiculous that a student who can barely keep his grades to the passing level could pull off something that requires so much discipline.

Owen tells me again that he believes me, and he believes I'm sorry. Then he suggests that we give the money found in Hallso's room to the church. I agree. After all, anything I can do to help not get kicked out of this place sounds like a great idea.

Hallso gets suspended for two weeks as this is his first strike. It's my second, after stealing the master key. Actually, it's probably my third or fourth, but it's the second time I've been caught, so second. The meeting is going to be held in the Archives, which makes this a big deal. Now I just have to get somebody to stand up for me. My student pick is easy: Skip. Skip and I have been friends since day one in Edith Hall. He's a great hockey player, a great student, and all-around, one of my closest friends. He's a team player and I'm selfish. He enjoys school and I repeated the fifth grade twice. We're total opposites, but good pals. I know the staff members will take him seriously as he's well respected in the Notre Dame community. I'll ask him later when I'm back in the dorm.

For my staff pick, I decide to ask Abe Solmon, the coach of the football team and the guy whose office I sat in at Maynard House earlier. Although I don't ever actually play during football games, I've never missed a practice. Abe's got a good relationship with the man upstairs, so I'm thinking maybe he can bring some mercy into my meeting. But when I ask him, he says he has to think about it. I know I'm asking him on the spot to vouch for me and I have no clue what they're going to ask him, but it kind of bothers me that he has to think about it.

"All right," he says, "I'll do it." This is great. Skip and Abe are the two best choices I could make. I go back to my dorm room, which I'm now confined to until the meeting. I wonder if this might be the last time I'm here. I have no clue what this meeting will bring. There's an army of guys gathered in my room, all my friends, asking me all sorts of questions. I tell everyone to calm down and whisper over to my roommate, Matty, that I need to speak with Skip. Matty kicks everyone out and motions to Skip to stay. Skip sits at a study desk, dangling his feet and kicking one of the chairs. I tell him what I need from him and that I understand if he wants to say no. He tells me that his dad wouldn't be too happy with him, but he doesn't care. He'll do it. Skip asks me what he needs to do to prepare, but the truth is, I have no idea.

"Just speak the truth, whatever they ask. That's all we can do," I say. We sort of brainstorm for a little while, and I'm trying to write something down to help him, some pointers, but it's just useless scribbles. I can't think well right now. "Meeting is tonight, I'll get you and we'll walk to the Archives."

I don't go for dinner or even drink anything. I just wait in my room. I'm a mess and I can't even sit still. I cry, and I laugh, and I get angry. I don't know how I'm supposed to feel right now. Finally, the time comes. I put on khaki pants and a dress shirt, trying to look like the reasonable young man I clearly am not. I yell up to Skip and we meet up, then head out of Max Bell. Skip's trying to loosen me up, whispering to me not to worry.

"Think positive," he says. "People have done worse, man. It's not as bad as you think."

Doubtful. When I walk into the Archives, there's a table full of people that I respect, but they probably don't like me. Most likely, they're all disgusted by what I've done. I sit down at the oval-shaped table surrounded by stone walls with figures sculpted into them. The lights are dimmed, and Faith, who's sitting across the table from me, asks if I'd like coffee, tea, or a snack. Based on my surroundings, I'm pretty sure this is not going to be a short meeting. If things weren't apparent before, they sure are now: I'm in deep fucking shit.

Chapter 19

Shattered

here are a lot of faculty members in the room, but only a few stand out to me. These are the ones I know are against me. What's the point? I can sing whatever sob story I want, but they're all tired of them. Faith, the principal's wife, addresses the meeting and thanks everybody for coming. She explains that after everybody has a chance to speak, there will be a vote to decide if I will be able to stay at school or be expelled. This is the first time I'm hearing this, and it's really starting to sink in that this is it. The conversation goes around the table with some staff speaking and others opting not to. It isn't all teachers there, either. Some of these people have simply been picked at random, and I'm not sure how they chose this group of so-called jurors. Some questions are directed at Skip, and he's offering answers and making promises that are completely absurd. He's trying to help me, but I feel like nothing he says makes any difference. It feels like a setup.

Skip says he's willing to take responsibility for any future troubles I get into and that he'll make sure I stay on track if they let me stay. They go into detail about my operation and what I've been doing, and Skip says he knows nothing about it. I'm impressed with how well Skip's doing, going on about how I've made a mistake, but everyone makes mistakes. When the staff members have no more questions for Skip, Terry O'Malley, the president of Notre Dame, decides it's his turn. Terry is a three-time Canada hockey Olympian who's respected by everyone— not just on campus, but everyone everywhere. He's one of the few people I truly admire and respect. He stands up to speak. I can't wait to hear what Terry has to say.

"Christos," he says, pointing at me, "you pissed on the college." I feel my heart shattering in a billion pieces, and I know that with my last dying breath, I'll never forget those words. O'Malley just knocked any hopes of staying at Notre Dame right out of me. And he isn't wrong.

A few more people talk, then Abe Solmon, the guy I asked to represent me, turns to me and says, "Well, Christos, I'm just not sure I'd like to represent you anymore." At that point, I guess it didn't matter if Abe turned his back on me—Terry had already thrown me out a closed glass window.

I'm finished. Here I am, I finally came clean and told my whole story, and I'm just asking for mercy. They have none. Maybe I shouldn't expect it, after all the pain, embarrassment, humiliation, and worst of all, shame I've brought on the school.

I've never taken a step back to assess the big picture until now. I love this place, but I've never realized how much until now, and I don't want to leave. None of that matters to these people; I can see in their eyes all the destruction I've caused, and any good I've done means nothing. Before the meeting ends, Faith asks if anyone would like to say anything else. I stand up and motion that I'd like to speak. I apologize for everything I've done and say that no matter what happens, I want to thank Faith and Owen for everything they've done for me. My heart's broken though; I can't believe how emotional I'm getting. They tell me and Skip we can go, and they'll have an answer for me by the end of the day. The wait is going to be pure hell.

Back in my room, Skip and some other guys who've been with us since grade nine are there, and we sit around and bullshit for a while, almost pretending like the meeting never happened. It's nice to spend time with these guys—whatever time I have left here. Later on, everyone clears out one by one, till it's just me and Skip.

"Hey man," he says. "Even if you get kicked out of here, what a story. I mean, don't think I'm not going to tell this story about the kid who had this entire school up in arms. Think about it, man. If you're going out, it's with a bang."

I like that. Skip always has a way to cheer me up, even in the worst situations. I lay down in my bed and doze off. It's much needed. I'm tired. That meeting in Maynard House seems like it happened so long ago, even though it was just this morning. And with all the stress, I've gotten less than three hours of sleep in the past two days. After what seems like just a few minutes, I hear the door open and a voice call out,

"Christos, get up and follow me, okay?"

It's Owen, and I follow him down to John Woodsmere's office, pounding him with questions the whole way. I feel like a kid who could be going to prison or Disneyland, and I don't know which.

"Am I staying? Are they letting me stay? Please tell me I'm staying." Owen doesn't crack. He keeps his cool and waits until we're on John's turf.

"Take a seat," John says.

"I'll stand," I reply. They look at me, then at one another with body language that says neither of them wants to be the one to break the news. Owen speaks the words that seem to take a lifetime to come out of his mouth.

"Christos, I'm sorry to tell you this..." I don't even let him finish. I'm crying hysterically. Between sobs, I ask if I can come back next year.

Owen says that if I stay out of trouble and get good grades back in Fort McMurray, he'll make it happen. At least there's some sort of silver lining, if you can call it that. John puts his hand out to give me something, and I think it's a tissue, but it's a cordless phone. I grab it from him and take it with me, leaving the room.

I sit on the carpeted steps that lead upstairs to the houseparents' office. Cradling the phone with both hands. I'm rocking back and forth, sobbing. I hear one of the houseparents yelling at the guys in the dorm, but I don't even care what's going on out there. My focus is on how I'm going to tell my mom that I just got expelled from Athol Murray College of Notre Dame. It takes me twenty minutes to muster up the courage to call.

My mother isn't surprised to hear from me, and she says that John had called her and told her about the meeting and that she knew they weren't going to let me stay. Even though she knew it was coming, I hear her crying on the other end of the phone. We're both crying now, my mom 650 miles away in Northern Alberta and me in the middle of nowhere, Saskatchewan. We both want nothing more than to turn back time. I know I've let her down, and there's nothing I can do to fix it.

After a long talk, with both of us telling the other one to stop crying, we end the call. I pick myself up and get out from under the stairwell, wiping my face with my hands. I turn the corner and John and Owen are standing there. They tell me that I won't be in lockdown for the night, but this is the last time I have to say goodbye to my friends. I know they don't have to grant me this gift, and I greatly appreciate it. These two guys, for all the grief I've caused them, look as sad as me, and I'm starting to understand that this is hard for them too. They've become my family over the years, and they don't like causing me pain, but it's out of their hands.

I call Sophie's house, and her mom answers. She puts Sophie on the phone, and she says she can sneak out and meet me in person so I can explain everything. We agree to meet up at the little white church in town. This will be different from all the other times Sophie and I have gotten together under the cover of darkness. I'll be happy to see her, of course, but I'm not expecting any joy or laughter.

I'm thankful that I'll get to see her and be able to tell her what happened before the news begins to circle across campus. I go to my room to grab my coat first, and there's a crowd of guys in my room, my dorm mates, and they want to know what happened.

I'm focused on Sophie, though, so I get my coat and make my way over to the church. I haven't told anybody except my mom, and now I have to tell Sophie. It's unbearably cold tonight, maybe even more so under the circumstances. I sit down on the steps of the church and try to stay calm; I don't want to be bawling my eyes out in front of my friend. Pretty soon, I see her walking up slowly. She can tell from my face that the news isn't good. I take a big breath.

She sits down right next to me, and before she says anything, I blurt out, "I've been expelled from Notre Dame, but I can come back next year if I don't screw up."

Sophie nods her head. "At least you can come back," she says. "Just don't screw up." We start to laugh.

"Yeah. I know, I know."

We sit and talk about how pissed my parents are going to be. We talk about other times that make me forget, for a little while, just how bad everything is for me right now. I thank Sophie for allowing me to escape. I tell her I'll see her tomorrow in Canada Park after Assembly so I can say goodbye to her and Emma.

Sophie walks back to her house, and I watch until I can't see her anymore. I sit there on the steps in the cold wind crying alone. It's hitting me all over again. I'm getting kicked out. I'm losing my friends. I'm losing my life. And I'm about to have this same conversation a dozen more times. I wanted to tell Sophie first because I knew she'd comfort me instead of cracking jokes like the boys will.

When I get back to the dorm, it's filled with friends. There's a lot of hugs and more tears. It sucks. I see Dennis Quill at the end of the hallway. He's the guy I promised that I wouldn't sell alcohol to his little brother, and I didn't. Dennis is crying, and I realize how many people I've let down—not just my family, but my friends, teachers, acquaintances, and classmates. I have to accept that I won't be around to share the memories or see the guys in the grade ahead of me graduate. I've been selfish. Matty and some of the other guys help me pack my stuff. Then I go around to all the rooms and say my last goodbyes.

***

It's the next morning, and John wakes me up to tell me the students have put signs up all over campus wishing me farewell. This means a lot, seeing all the banners and signs people put up about not forgetting me. The teachers are already removing them because they don't want to glorify my departure. I check out the signs, then I go back to my room and say goodbye to my closest friends who are all there to send me off. These guys have been with me from the start.

John comes into my room and says that after Assembly, I could take a taxi to the airport, but he's volunteered to take me. "I figured you'd appreciate that overtaking a long silent cab ride."

After Assembly, I walk over to Canada Park where I say my final goodbyes to Sophie and Emma, complete with hugs and sobs.

As John and I exit the campus, I see girls and boys of all ages waving to me from different classrooms on either side of Main Street, in McCusker and Carr Halls. Some of my friends are laughing and giving me the middle finger in an attempt to make me laugh. This is the hardest part of all. I don't even want to look. It's too upsetting.

Just as we pass Maynard House, John slows the car and I see Owen and Faith. I get out of the car, and Faith hugs me so tight, her nails dig into my winter coat and Owen has to pull her off me. I don't know if she's crying because I got kicked out or because she thinks she failed me. I know she's given her all with me and then some, and I've still come up short.

Chapter 20

Vindication

ooking back at my time at Notre Dame, I kind of realized how much I took for granted. Even the bad parts weren't as bad as I thought. Rodeo Day, for example, seemed like a cruel initiation. But no one ever got seriously hurt. No one was trying to kill anybody. I doubt, though, in these times, that they still let things run wild like they did back then. I also realize that I was a troublemaker who sometimes took it too far, but I didn't mean any harm, at least not at first. I was just an adolescent finding my way like most do.

I wish I had never lost Terry's knife. It really meant something to him, and I feel bad for not taking care of it. I wish I would have appreciated the experience with him and his wife Eleanor even more when I stayed with them on the Farm. It's the same with Owen and Faith, and even John. Even Chief, who I couldn't stand back then, was just trying to mold us to be better versions of ourselves. Those people may have given me a hard time, but they cared about what happened to me. I just didn't see it at the time. I've figured out since then that having people truly care about you is a rare thing and you should never take it for granted.

I did go back to Notre Dame, but not right away. I went home to Fort McMurray and tried homeschooling for a while. That was a disaster. So my parents put me in a local high school. I got my grades up to where they needed to be and finished eleventh grade. Then I went back to Notre Dame to do my last year of high school. I knew it wouldn't be the same, but I wanted to see my old friends again. I wanted to prove I could finish, not just for me, but for Owen, and Faith, and my parents too. Finally, I received my diploma from Athol Murray College of Notre Dame.

Eventually, I joined the school's alumni advisory board. My first meeting as a board member was in that same room where the staff interrogated me about my liquor operation. I sat in the same seat as the one I sat in when Skip defended me, where Terry said I pissed on the school, and where the staff decided to expel me. It felt a lot different sitting there this time. I was dressed in a suit, and I felt good. Not scared or helpless. Not like I was at the mercy of a bunch of adults who didn't even know me. I felt in control. Like a man. A few years ago, they named me Alumnus of the Year. I got an award.

I've let go of all the anger I had against the people who, at the time, I thought had screwed me. In hindsight, most of them likely had my best interests at heart. There are no bad feelings or personal vendettas. It took me years to get there, though.

I love this place. Notre Dame and Wilcox. And Saskatchewan, for that matter. It's a place and an experience unlike any other. It's known as a big-time hockey school with a lot of Olympians to its credit. Some of them are my buddies. But it's so much more than that. We all love this place. I'll take it with me wherever I go. It keeps a piece of you once you've left.

I know now that I've never fully valued my time at Notre Dame, but it's had a massive impact on me. And I like to think that, on some level, I've had an impact on it. Over the years, I've been called a legend because of what I did there. The teachers may not admit it, and even the residents of the town may deny it. It happened.

Nobody ever asked me what I think about it. Even though many loved hearing the story, I'd love to tell you that, truthfully, it was one big well-planned terrible idea. And I wouldn't change it for the world.

Epilogue

ome people can prosper and achieve with minimal help from others. Many people tried to get through to me with guidance and support. For a while, I was a lost cause. I had a large, sharp chip on my shoulder that was, thankfully, over time, smoothed out and turned into motivation. I was a four-year Hound, and Père Murray's views and ideological seeds were planted deep inside me. Through the years away from home, living in Wilcox, through good times and bad, not one staff member ever gave up on me, even those who didn't actually teach me a class or coach me in a sport.

Compared to the outside world, I found the culture of lifting people's spirits amongst the student body at Notre Dame much more noticeable. I saw many students from rough back-grounds—First Nation reserves, inner-city youth, students from broken families, etc.—become molded into something special. My own parents, at the time, didn't have the extra money to send me to a boarding school, which is not cheap, no matter the institution. Looking back, I now see that the room, board, and endless hours that teachers spent sacrificing their own personal family time to further teach academically struggling students like myself are unrepayable.

In retrospect, I neglected to value my time while there. I wouldn't say that a specific moment or a revelation later in life opened my eyes and showed me the need to distance myself from negative environments and situations, but it was rather a slow awakening. I met good and bad people at Notre Dame; the bad ones either got kicked out very early or were able to work with people there to help them mature into the best version of themselves. For me, this meant identifying who I wanted to become and returning to the school years later to work toward that goal.

I began writing this book after graduation. At the time, I was not a big reader. I read the book *I Hope They Serve Beer in Hell* by Tucker Max and thought to myself, "If this guy wrote a book, so could I."

I worked on this book on and off for years. While discussing the details of what happened with people from my past, and people

I didn't even know, many asked if the story about selling booze in water bottles was actually even true. It was, and though explaining it was comical at times, I found myself repeating myself a lot as I corrected the details of what people knew, or thought they knew.

Now that I have written it down, I hope you enjoy my story as much as I enjoyed living it.

Acknowledgments

Thanks first to my family.

To my sister and brother, thanks for being older than me so I could study how to get away with drastically more than either of you ever did. I guess this is payback for all the times we sat and played video games and I was handed a controller that wasn't in play, yet I didn't find out about it till several years later. Good times. Maharajah 1, 5, 2, 2, 6 / Egypt 1 Sun 2 Moon 3 Star. It took years off our lives, but we finally got there.

To my father, whose story is far more incredible than my own. I learn more from you as time goes by.

To my mom, who chose hosting my friends and me for my fifth birthday party over your only chance to see Whitney Houston in concert, during the "I'm Your Baby Tonight World Tour" (May 3, 1991). If that's not love, I don't know what is.

To both of my parents, I know you didn't have the money to send me to Notre Dame, but you did, and no amount of money could ever repay that.

To everyone back in Fort Mac. (NOW THAT'S A STORY.)

To the entire team at Scribe. Susan, I'm beyond humbled and lucky to get to have worked with you. Thanks for trying it my way. To Nat, the best project manager there is. To Miles, the energy almost broke my computer screen, brother—nothing but positive thoughts. And to everyone involved with the cover and all the staff behind the scenes. Words can't describe the incredible experience this has been. Looking forward to the next one! And last and certainly not least, thanks to Tucker Max. Reading your book all those years ago inspired me to start writing. In a million years, I never would have thought you would be the one who signed me to write mine. I'd be lying if I told you there wasn't a tear coming down my face right now. Big things coming.

To everyone at Notre Dame for making all these stories possible. To all the staff and students—way too many to thank individually, but you know who you are. A very special thank you to Doug

Branchflower, and to a husband and wife who never gave up on me, Darren Olson and Shirley Olson, may she rest peacefully. I don't think I would be alive if it weren't for your guidance.

To John and Maureen Power, your mentorship is immeasurable. And to the entire Schwartz family, thanks for believing in the vision. Lots to come. Save me a spot at the bar, Rick; until then, I'll keep my promise.

About the Author

One of the most notorious graduates of the storied Athol Murray College of Notre Dame, Christos Kalogirou is an author, entrepreneur, and philanthropist. His story is one of a classic comeback. A former alumni board member and the recipient of the 2014 National Alumnus of the Year, Christos dedicates his time to his various businesses, along with raising valuable resources for non-profits, especially the Mandi Schwartz Foundation and Hockey Gives Blood.

Christos Kalogirou is the only student in the history of Athol Murray College of Notre Dame, which was founded in 1920, to be expelled from the school, return, graduate, and be awarded Alumnus of the Year.

Endnotes

Endnotes provided by Terry O'Malley, who was the president of Athol Murray College of Notre Dame from 2003–2006. I am proud to call Terry my friend.

[1] A residential area was developed in the town of Wilcox. Many teachers built homes there, and parents came to live in town in order to avail a private school education and the programs within it. The Schwartzes mentioned in the story did that while the family commuted to Regina for work. Other residents did the same. Some were farmers who moved into town or worked locally. Former students of the college moved to Wilcox too. The fees were substantial. (It became such a popular thing to do that the college had to change the fee structure for local students.) There were about twenty-five to thirty town students at the college while Christos attended Athol Murray, and of course they had a nickname: "town rats" or "townies." There were a few students who came from the nearby towns of Rouleau and Milestone. The town Wilcox was named after the first rail station master. It has a service road, a municipal office and maintenance building, post office, a small bentonite (used for make-up and oil drilling), clay plant, one grain elevator, a Catholic church, a closed-down United Church, public grade school #1633 with a playground, small motel/restaurant, a railway track across the highway with its co-op depot, and a dump. The rest of the town was filled with school buildings. It was built like all the towns along the rail line in grid

fashion, every eight miles apart. Only the main street is paved, and considering the mud when it rained, that was a big deal when it happened in the 1950s. The town got its water from an underground river and was sourced from the next town, Rouleau, sixteen miles west of Wilcox. It was plentiful. Apparently, it has enough flow to service a city the size of Toronto continuously for ten years. However, it is alkaline because there are large underground deposits of potash throughout Saskatchewan. People could get kidney stones from it. This water reputation gave cover to the water bottle enterprise of Christos. A 2016 census recorded a population of 264 living in eighty of Wilcox's ninety-three total private dwellings.

[2] Jack Gorman, Père Murray and the Hounds: The Story of Saskatchewan's Notre Dame College (Calgary: Johnson Gorman, 1990).

[3] Varsity Hall was built in 1958. It was part of an effort by alumni to move out of wooden buildings and into permanent "brick and mortar" edifices. The rector, Athol Murray, with his connections, and alumni were able to scrounge a grant from the federal government to assist in its construction. Also, because of an endowment of $100,000 left to the college by famous American adventurer and author, Rex Beach, who did articles on the college in the 1930s and '40s, enough funds were procured. Varsity was the name of the hall because the college at that time had a thriving liberal arts college, an affiliate to the University of Ottawa. It became a gathering point for meals, movie nights, banquets, and also assemblies each morning, where news was shared. In Assembly, students learned all the results from the last evening's events and learned about upcoming ones. In Assembly, each day began with the anthem, prayer, and reflection. Varsity Hall was also the scene of a notorious food fight. Varsity Hall was a "big deal" addition to the college, and Rex Beach was recognized in a legacy room. New students were sometimes asked, as a prank, to go wake him up in the morning. This room was moved to the Archives during Christos's time there.

[4] There is an actual "4-mile" road, which is a shortcut to the college off Highway 06 out of Regina. One does not use it when it is raining heavily because it turns into greasy mud—the gumbo that allows for some of the best cereal crop farming in the world because it holds moisture. The area of Wilcox is geographically assigned as "semi-desert" because it only gets twelve to fifteen inches of rain a year. This mud makes the difference and helps short people grow —two to three inches if you walk in it. There is also another backroad "4-mile" route that is used for the annual autumn Terry Fox run to raise money for cancer research.

[5] The area between Regina and Wilcox is designated on some official maps as the flattest territory in the world. The only turn in the road is called a "correction line" because the surveyed latitude line curves into the North Pole. The area is called the Palliser Triangle and named after John Palliser, an Irish geographer who, in 1857 with a number of scientists, led an expedition to survey and conclude if the area was suitable for settlement. The area of Wilcox was then considered too dry for farming, but this was later proved wrong because of the ability of the clay to hold moisture. But it did lead to Western Canada being purchased by the Government of Canada in 1869 from the Hudson's Bay Company. Truly, you can see thirty miles to the horizon in all

directions. When the fields are changing color from green to gold, purple, or yellow, it is a magnificent sight. Otherwise, it can be quite barren with farm yards and grain elevators as the only contrast around. I was driving a Japanese student from the airport to the college one time. He was excited to be there. By the time we were halfway to the college, he had slunk down in his seat so that his eyes could barely see over the dash of the car. It's that flat. (He ended up staying four years.)

⁶ The Hound Shop was the college store for supplies and college wear and gifts. Of course, "Hounds" was the nickname for students.

⁷ Canada Park was introduced during the Canadian Separation Crisis in 1995 when the Province of Quebec had a referendum whether or not to separate from Canada. Plaques were made for each province and territory. It was an attempt to rally the student body and surrounding populations that the idea of keeping Canada together was a worthy one.

⁸ The football and baseball fields were built out behind the old rink in the northwest part of the town. They were developed there in the 1990s because of the water supply in dugouts. It is in a low-lying area of the campus, and winter snow runoff would be caught in the dugouts. It has small stands to watch baseball. It is where fall and spring sports and activities happen. The cemetery is at the opposite southeast end of the town and campus. It goes back to the founding of the town in 1907. Many of the local farmers, staff, and students of Notre Dame are buried there. As was part of the early sectarian times, the cemetery is divided into Catholic and Protestant sections and is looked after nicely by the town maintenance person. I think at Halloween, the students used to work out some pranks there, but I can't recall just what.

⁹ The college was always trying to upgrade its structures. The new link, built in the 1990s, attached two dormitories, Fred Hill and Max Bell. It provided a lounge area and a place to store boots. Also, the link allowed students to travel between dormitories without going outside.

¹⁰ The Tower of God was an idea of college rector Père Athol Murray. He deplored religious sectarianism and secular humanism. His was a God-centered or, as philosopher Jacques Maritain called it, "authentic" humanist. The Tower of God was a practical expression of a hope for humanity to overcome prejudices. It recognized that the common root of the three great monotheistic religions, Judaism, Islam, and Christianity, had their same roots in Abraham. The Tower of God was built in 1960, as Israel and the Arab States were at war. Athol Murray tried to introduce his ideas to the Middle East, when he visited Jerusalem and Saudi Arabia. Recent accords between Arab States and Israel are called the Abraham Accords. Visit the college's website for a virtual tour of the campus, the Archives, and the Tower of God.